A General Theory Of Acquisitivity

A General Theory Of Acquisitivity

On Human Nature, Productivity and Survival

Wayne Jett

Writer's Showcase presented by *Writer's Digest*
San Jose New York Lincoln Shanghai

A General Theory Of Acquisitivity
On Human Nature, Productivity and Survival

Published by Writer's Showcase presented by *Writer's Digest* an imprint of iUniverse.com, Inc.

For information address:
iUniverse.com, Inc.
620 North 48th Street
Suite 201
Lincoln, NE 68504-3467
www.iuniverse.com

ISBN: 0-595-09602-6

Printed in the United States of America

Dedication

This book is dedicated to my father, A. E. Jett, to my mother, Zettia Davis Jett, and to their children, each of whom contributed importantly to making the best of times from what might have been otherwise.

Acknowledgments

I want to thank my friend John Edmundson for his encouragement in early conversations, years ago, to believe that my thoughts on the natural mechanism for resource allocation were significant and ought to be developed in detail.

My special thanks to Joyce Meadows, one of my dear sisters, for her helpful assistance in preparing, reading and proofing the manuscript, for her daily good humor and for her courage in all things that matter.

And I am especially grateful to my wife, Jane, for her confidence in the worthiness of my efforts to contribute, and for the time to be thoughtful about ideas that may be important in the longer term.

Contents

Creating A World

Imagine you are creating a world. What would your world be like?

The idea of a world, of course, suggests something existing in a place. Being in a location. So, first your imagination might deal with the place of your world. For instance, you might have a generally round ball moving at a comfortable distance around a relatively stationary source of heat and light. Maybe you would call the heat-light source the "sun."

Now that you have a place in mind, what would you imagine should exist there? Maybe something solid to start, so you could have a platform for further work. Call it "firmament" or the "ground" or whatever you please, but the imagination does not readily yield an alternative concept for a world base of operations. That is, unless you have a better idea.

Everything in the world being solid is a little dull and limiting, though, don't you think? So you would likely want to add variety and flexibility in the form of fluid or liquid matter to fill in the cracks and crevices of the solid. And then something even lighter and vaporous to hover around the solid and liquids. You begin to grasp the concept that the mind does not readily yield ideas in the realm of world creation more imaginative or miraculous than those we observe around us.

But this world creation business can be a lot of fun, too. Once you get going, you might have your "ground" or "earth" with lots of "water" around. And even though you made the water a clear liquid with no color, you put it in lots of different locations and use the light from the sun to give it a range of colors as time and surroundings change. Not a bad touch on your part.

Now that you are on a roll, you might be ready for a whole new concept to spring from your imagination. The idea that something in your world should not be permanent, but should come and go periodically. Call it a "living" thing. Start with living things attached to the solid ground. Trees, grass—that begins to make the place look a little more interesting and "lived in." And how about something really pretty to look at by itself—flowers! Now that's a great idea!

With such a terrific "place" to "be" already laid out, and living things playing an active role in your world, you are definitely ready for the big step towards the creation of something living that could move around and act on its own. Such creatures as this could be so animated as to be companions with each other, to reproduce themselves, to eat the grass and other plants that otherwise seem to overgrow the place. That would provide a sort of "balance" to keep the plants in check.

Come to think of it, the animals probably will need some "checking" of the same kind, or else they will overrun the place in no time. So you undoubtedly will expand on that idea as you go along to achieve something of a "balance of nature" in your world.

But right now, it is just too much fun—downright exhilarating, in fact—to think up all of these great little touches to get this new world hopping. An eagle. A lion. A zebra. A fish. Lots of different fishes, of every color and shape, to be in the water. Horses! Bluebirds! What a trip!!

And quite an achievement. Such tremendous energy, beauty, competition, complexity and simplicity, all within a system that seems to keep working and replenishing itself automatically, once you set it in motion.

If the truth be known, your creativity far exceeds even the truly remarkable innovations mentioned so far. Indeed, the descriptions given are no more than a kindergarten view of the levels of complexity in your world.

You have used an invisible attractive force to hold your world together and to hold your world in place in relation to the sun. You have given all matter a degree of commonality in the design of the very smallest particles comprising it. You have created organisms so small as to be invisible to the most powerful animals roaming your world, and yet capable of attacking and killing those magnificent prey.

Still, with all of that truly astounding creativity under your belt, you might yearn for something more. Something on the order of a crowning achievement. Or, if not a crowning achievement, at least something that runs across the grain of this balance of nature thing. After all, you can only go so far with designing millions of species, each of which fits somewhere in a chain, controlling certain species and supporting others. What kind of a creation might add a significantly different ingredient to that mix?

What about something in the nature of a human being? This would be a creature in many respects like other animals you have made. In some ways, the human would be just another link in the chains you have made of plants and other animals. But the main distinction would be instilling or implanting in the human a greater capacity for that facility you, yourself, have displayed so well: creativity. The ability to innovate. Imagination! Who knows where that might lead? Certainly seems to add considerable doses of spice and mystery, wouldn't you agree?

Let's consider some of the potential ramifications of creating a human being. A being with the individual capacity for innovation could devise ways to overcome even the most fearsome of the animals stalking the world. In time, the human being might think of ways to avoid, if not overcome, the forces of nature which, at the outset, would appear to be insurmountable obstacles to his success and survival. If that should prove to be the case, then what could possibly stand in the way of practical domination of the entire world you have created by this newly conceived human being? Nothing that comes immediately to mind.

If the human being becomes the dominant species, so what? Maybe not much, at least for quite a while. Humans could live pretty close to the food chain of nature, like other animals for a long time, perhaps hundreds or even millions of years. Famine, disease—you know the various scenarios.

But if this imagination thing begins to come to grips with reality in meaningful ways, humans could actually arrive at a time of widespread success against their foes. When that occurs, humans would multiply their own numbers to such an extent as to overpopulate the world, crowding out plants and animals, and expending all the resources available and necessary even for their own sustenance.

Come to think of it, these human beings could, by their own nature, be the cause of their own eventual demise. They might even cause the destruction of the world you have spent so much effort (and imagination) creating. Not a very comforting outcome for this exciting new human being you are proposing to create and introduce into your world.

But with innovation, imagination and thinking capacity installed (or instilled) in each individual human, is it not possible that an infinite number of other potentially better outcomes could be achieved? What if, for example, you created humans with different talents, varying capabilities and interests, some of whom could produce more than others?

Then, perhaps, you could imagine some way to bring the most resources to the individual humans who could be the most productive with those resources. That would seem to have the effect of greatly increasing the chances of success in overcoming this dilemma about overpopulation by the dominant species.

Just a thought, and probably too farfetched to be practical in this human creation project. After all, who could imagine a way of providing more resources to the specific individual humans best able to be productive with them?

Nah, too farfetched. Probably wouldn't work. But then again…

One | Acquisitivity In Human Nature

"More."

So answered Walter P. Reuther after his election in 1946 as president of the United Auto Workers, when asked what his members wanted.[1] Simple, concise and direct, yet deeply insightful and respectful in communicating the breadth of the desire among industrial workers to acquire wealth of every kind.

Reuther might as well have been describing the motivation driving Henry Ford or J. Paul Getty during their long careers devoted to building enormously productive capitalist enterprises. Ford and Getty are representative of countless others who have continued to work hard at their economic activities long after their personal fortunes exceeded the needs of all future generations of their respective families.

The commonality of motivations among workers and owners of American business enterprises is not particularly surprising. In the mere eleven score and four years since the Declaration of Independence adopted the principle that all men are created equal, evolutionary processes could not have produced significant genetic differences between those who employ and those who are employed. Any perceived differences between employers and employees would arise from cultural influences, not natural characteristics.

The perception that humans have equal entitlement to respect for their rights by government is not the equivalent of deeming their individual motivations and natural character to be uniform. Other fundamental principles announced and protected in the American Constitution were specifically designed with the individual's right to be different in mind.

The Founders of the Constitution understood that one of the fundamental ways in which individuals differ is in their capabilities to acquire property. Indeed, the history of the American colonies shows that much of what underlay the "unalienable right" given by God to each individual to "the pursuit of happiness" was a widely held belief in the sacred entitlement of each person to pursue the acquisition and ownership of property.

The precise origin or content of these principles and beliefs in American history is not the point at issue here. The challenge at hand is to understand better the nature and purpose of the human desire to acquire and own property. Is acquisitiveness a "capitalist tendency" within certain people produced by particular types of cultural development, or is it something more deeply engrained in human nature?

Certainly Americans have no exclusive call upon acquisitiveness as a feature of individual character. The ideas reflecting understanding of human nature that inspired American constitutional government were gleaned by the Founding Fathers from primarily European intellectual sources. But wherever a careful examination is made, whether in China, India, South or Central America, Africa or Australia, the human desire to acquire is identifiable in the general populace as a commonly displayed characteristic.

The primary differences noticeable among people in wide-ranging geographic locales seem to be attributable to the manner in which governments have dealt with man's acquisitive nature. Some governments and religions have attempted to stifle individual acquisition of property, while others have permitted it to flourish, at least to varying degrees. Often the actions of governments in this respect have been influenced by the desires of organized religions.

For example, governments of countries in which the Islamic faith is predominant have given particular attention to the regulation of banking activities such as money lending, due to the religious precept that charging interest is wrong. Many Western governments levy "progressively" higher tax rates on higher incomes of individuals and businesses. This public policy is based upon a premise derived at least in part from Christian theological arguments (both Catholic and Protestant in origin) that disparity in income levels should be minimized and wealth should be redistributed more uniformly than occurs absent government intervention.

The American Catholic intellectual and philosopher Michael Novak has contended that three "dynamic and converging systems functioning as one" are required for a democratic capitalist society to survive and thrive. The three systems are: political democracy, a market economy and pluralistic moral-cultural system.[2] Novak argues further that democracy is fundamentally linked with the market economy because democracy is incompatible with any other economic system. Yet, as Novak then proceeds to show quite persuasively, both Catholic and Protestant theologies have displayed varying degrees of hostility towards capitalism and market economies, and harsh conclusions have been passed along in the teaching of clergy and the faithful.[3]

Indeed, much of what government does with respect to economic affairs in the so-called modern welfare state is directed towards modifying the effects of property acquisition that otherwise transpires through private conduct. This being the case, the search for a better understanding of the true nature of man's acquisitive character takes on greater significance.

If this acquisitiveness is a part of the natural makeup of humans, then perhaps a good reason exists for its presence. And, if that is so, then the actions of governments directed towards thwarting the free exercise of this human characteristic might, in fact, be counter-productive rather than helpful to social and economic progress.

Certainly the lessons of history, including particularly the Twentieth Century, leave no reason for confidence that governments already have all the right answers, or are incapable of acting in ways very harmful to their own people and to others. Thus, even at such a late date as the present, when the "end of history" in the evolution of government may be at hand, perhaps some degree of enlightenment can still be found to improve the outcomes people around the world will otherwise experience when interfacing with their governments. This seems to be a worthwhile purpose for thoughtful pursuit.

That being said, examination of the human proclivity to acquire property is an exercise that has not been overdone in recent times. In America, perhaps partially due to political partisanship built upon class envy, all aspects of acquisitiveness are generally lumped into the single category of a moral concept called "greed." Upon closer examination, however, when people of relatively meager means are involved, their efforts to acquire property are more generously termed "getting ahead" and "working hard." Thus, the pejorative term "greed" is most commonly applied only when a person already having relatively sizeable assets seeks to acquire more property, or when a poor person aspires to acquire a lot of property.

Surprisingly, the English language has not yet produced a word or even a term of art that easily and sufficiently describes this "natural human proclivity to acquire." Words describing other human characteristics abound, some involving considerably less notable and consequential aspects of individual manner and conduct. Sensibility and sensitivity, among many others, come to mind as words serving perfectly useful purposes in communicating and understanding particular aspects of human nature. *Acquisitivity* is, therefore, a word whose time to be introduced into the English common vocabulary has long since arrived.

In historical perspective, acquisitivity is closely associated with political ideas that form the very core of Western democratic culture. Liberty, or individual and social freedom, depends in very important ways upon the success of acquisitivity.

A person cannot be truly free of the state's desires and demands unless he has, or is able to acquire, property sufficient to provide for the welfare of himself and his dependents. Consider the subservience to the state of a person who has just been, or is about to be, rendered a pauper by means of a governmental taking of his property. In a very practical sense, unless a person has property that cannot be taken from him by the government "without just compensation" as provided in the Fifth Amendment of the U.S. Constitution, that person is ultimately a ward of the state.

Beyond the realm of political ideas and the arrangement of government, however, is the more fundamental concern for survival of the species and the role of acquisitivity in that struggle. The motivation to acquire property may be inherently a part of human nature, divinely inspired in creation to serve as a potential key to the door of survival. Or, alternatively, the motivation to acquire property may be a trait of the "fittest" who have survived by and through their efforts to live long enough to reproduce.

Some would argue, undoubtedly, that regardless of whether the instinct to acquire is a God given characteristic, an evolved trait or a socially inspired ethic, the importance of acquisitivity is not diminished. That issue may deserve further debate. However, the point that should be fully appreciated, but often is not, is that the acquisitive nature of mankind is absolutely central to his prospects for survival.

The acquisitive activities of individual human beings is the most powerful, dynamic, diverse and persistent mechanism in existence for the allocation, distribution and use of resources for production of necessary goods and services. By the guidance of billions of independent and self-interested minds, voluntary transactions occur which bring additional resources to those who are better able to use them in the most creative and productive ways. The importance of this tremendously energetic and efficient mechanism in enhancing the potential for economic success of human society cannot be overstated.

Regardless of the desirability of optimism or the necessity of pessimism, and the many reasons for either, in assessing the prospects for the success of humans over the long term, the potential for human success is, at best, a tremendously difficult economic struggle. Over the short and intermediate terms, the challenges and failures of that economic struggle are exposed in the occurrences of famine, disease, war, genocide and similar afflictions that have accompanied the unparalleled prosperity of the Twentieth Century. But leaving the long term aside, even the intermediate term outlook foretells challenges unparalleled in human history.

Population growth has been a focus of concern in academic circles since the early Nineteenth Century, when the population of Europe began to grow more robustly. The population of France increased from 28.3 million in 1800 to 37.7 million in 1870. Germany grew from 20 million to 41.1 million over the same interval, and Italy from 17.2 million to 26 million. Britain increased in population most rapidly, from 10.5 million to 26 million, nearly tripling its numbers within those 70 years.[4]

However valid or invalid the concerns for population growth were in 1870, they could barely imagine the conditions present in the world as it turns into the Twenty First Century. From the beginning of human history until 1804, the world's population grew to one billion. Two billion was reached 123 years later, in 1927. Adding another 50 percent to reach three billion required only 33 years, to 1960, four billion was reached in 1974, and five billion in 1987. By the year 2000, world population will be above six billion and counting. That is billion, not million. Although we have become accustomed to speaking in such numbers when money is the subject, we should not be so complacent when each digit represents a human being who will spend a lifetime on the Earth.

Consumption of oil has risen from a few thousand barrels per day in 1900 to about 72 million barrels per day in 1999. Use of metals has risen from roughly 20 million tons per year to 1.2 billion tons per year over the same period. World grain production remains at just under two billion tons per year. Further details of the problem can be readily assembled, but the dimensions of world population growth undoubtedly define a challenge that is entirely real, a clear and present danger to all hopes for the future success of humanity.

In circumstances so dire and consequential as these, attention ought to be given to any opportunity for an advantage to be gained in this economic struggle. The possibility that an engine of creativity and productivity exists within each member of the human population in the form of a natural instinct to acquire property comprises such a tremendous prospect that its implications ought to be examined fully.

In 1776, Adam Smith wrote of the unintended, good social consequences flowing from the self-interested transactions of individuals in his book *An Inquiry Into The Nature And Causes Of The Wealth of Nations.* During the period of roughly 150 years thereafter, England was the dominant economic and military power in the world.[5] This circumstance resulted largely from the success of that relatively small country in achieving an average economic growth rate during that period of approximately two percent per year. England's growth came, not from the plunder of war or the mining of natural resources as had been the traditional monarchical roads to greater wealth, but from the release of individual human energies within a developing market economy.

The mechanism of human acquisitivity is central to the efficiency of the free market in the production of goods and services. This ought to be so self-evident as to be a truism. Yet, if that is so, then why is acquisitivity so often viewed in public discourse with disdain, rather than cherished and nurtured? Indeed, the premise ordinarily advanced as the best argument to be made for capitalism is the "greed is good" philosophy of the protagonist in the book and motion picture *The Bonfire of the Vanities.*[6] This is a serious misconception of both economic and moral principles.

Appreciation of the profound significance of acquisitivity in the economic order of the free market may be most easily gained by imagining the effects upon society if somehow human nature caused the opposite outcomes of our common experience. Specifically, imagine that the more a person works, the fewer resources he would have. The most creative and productive persons among us would become poorer and poorer until totally impoverished. On the other hand, those least willing or able to contribute to the production of food, clothing, shelter or other needs of society would somehow come into possession of the greatest quantities of material goods. Clearly, such an environment would have no hope at all of achieving productive output sufficient to sustain an expanding population of a dominant species, such as human beings are.

In stark contrast to such a dismal outlook, the market economies of the modern world are looking towards achieving within the foreseeable future expanded wealth and prosperity beyond the dreams of those who lived only a few generations ago. Karl Marx himself recognized with clarity, and near incredulity, the dramatic increase in prosperity in capitalist societies during the very short time they had existed when he observed:

"The bourgeoisie, during its rule of scarce one hundred years, has created more massive and more colossal productive forces than have all preceding generations together. Subjection of Nature's forces to man, machinery, application of chemistry to industry and agriculture, steam-navigation, railways, electric telegraphs, clearing of whole continents for cultivation, canalization of rivers, whole populations conjured out of the ground—what earlier century had even a presentiment that such productive forces slumbered in the lap of social labor?"[7]

Had Marx written in 2000 rather than 1848, how much more he might add to that already impressive catalog of bridges built from the Dark Ages into modernity! Consider, for example, airplanes, high-rise construction, nuclear energy, rocketry and space travel, radio and television, computers, modern medicine, genetics, satellite communications, the internet. The list could go on and on, and will undoubtedly do so at an ever increasing pace.

The monumental significance of acquisitivity in human nature begins to be illuminated when you compare this almost unimaginably productive, innovative and creative environment with the scenario described earlier in which "the opposite" of human acquisitivity prevails. On the one hand, the imagined society in which resources flow to the slow, the lazy, the feeble, the incapable or the uninspired, and *away from the productive,* the innovative, the energetic and the hard working is a society with no hope for long term success. On the other hand, the society we are experiencing directly, in which individuals are allowed varying degrees of freedom to exercise their creative talents, is presenting a dazzling display of wealth creation and economic growth nearly beyond the comprehension of even those who presently live in its midst.

Acquisitivity is, in a figurative but real and practical sense, the flip side of the coin of human productivity. Productivity is often praised, and understandably so, because it is easily recognized as the fountainhead from which economic growth flows. But productivity can grow only to the extent of its available resources, and that is where the mechanism of acquisitivity is essential.

Acquisitivity obtains resources to feed production. Production, in turn, then feeds acquisitivity. Neither can be successful without the other, at least not in the mid- to long term.

If an individual acquires resources and fails to use them productively, those resources can only be hoarded or consumed and eventually will be dissipated. However, resources acquired and put to productive use will be multiplied until the productive process fails. Without acquisitivity, productivity has little or no utility. Production will promptly cease when immediately available resources are consumed absent replenishment. The conclusion is self-evident that productivity cannot flourish, either in an individual enterprise or in the macro-economy, unless acquisitivity is equally successful.

This being the case, much closer attention ought to be given to understanding and nurturing the desire to acquire which exists in human nature. Relying upon "an increasing body of evidence coming out of the life sciences…that human beings are born with pre-existing cognitive structures and age-specific capabilities for learning that lead them naturally into society…," the American thinker Francis Fukuyama observes that "there is, in other words, such a thing as human nature." He further notes that "a tremendous amount of new work" on the level of macro-behavioral research suggests that "certain behavioral patterns are much more general than previously believed."[8]

One can hardly imagine a more generalized or more important behavioral pattern than the human proclivity to acquire. The prospect seems logical and probable, therefore, that acquisitivity qualifies as an inherent characteristic of human nature.

Scientific studies of laboratory mice by medical researchers at the University of Washington in Seattle and at Cambridge University in England have reported the identification of a gene that controls the release of hormonal substances within the mother of newborns. These substances, in turn, instill the "mothering instinct" in the parent that is so essential to the nurturing and survival of the infant offspring. David

Weinshenker of the University of Washington and Azim Surani of Cambridge University have reported that removal of the gene from the female mouse leaves the mother with no sense of responsibility for the care of her babies.

Already early reports indicate that similar DNA has been identified in humans. Is it likely that such genetic design is the result of learned cultural needs, or more probable that such genetics were inherent in the species as it originated? Regardless of its origin, the genetic design that comprises the living being is a part of nature without the need for cultural influence or intervention.

If similar genetic design can be found in humans, and a "mothering" gene is eventually isolated, the moral and social implications of potential genetic manipulation are profoundly significant for relations between parents and children. Even slight revision of the balance between parental love and the independence of offspring threatens family stability, with implications of the most far-reaching effects upon the prospects for success of entire populations.

Assuming a "mothering" gene exists, nonetheless, the prospects for a genetic design linked to acquisitivity in humans seem to be quite high. Of course, such a genetic design would make the case for acquisitivity as an inherent characteristic of human nature. In itself, this development would be significant in the discussion of acquisitivity and how it should be regarded in social culture. If the desire to acquire is built into human nature, is it to be regarded as a tendency towards sin and, accordingly, repressed by a righteous person? Or, as a basic characteristic of human nature, should acquisitivity be freely exercised?

The views of Sigmund Freud have radically changed Western societies during the Twentieth Century. The change has stemmed largely from Freud's contention that sexual desires and the libido, being elements of human nature, should be freely exercised rather than repressed or inhibited. Psychoanalysis has customarily treated certain frequently occurring psychological problems in terms of the natural libido and its excessive repression by society.

Whether Freud was essentially correct in his basic premise is still fairly questioned. Yet government and public policy have given very wide berth to Freud's premise that sexual practices, being a product of innate human nature, are fundamentally a matter of individual discretion that should not be required to conform to specified norms. Yes, governmental edicts control such highly objectionable conduct as incest, rape and child molestation. But a substantial public consensus appears to exist that government must "stay out of the bedroom" despite what arguably are significant public interests in such subjects as illegitimate pregnancy and the spread of disease. Of course, Freud is not necessarily responsible for this public sentiment. However, public policy has undoubtedly been influenced by Freud's view that repression of "natural" sexual desires produces important personality imbalances.

If the human personality is subject to harmful warping by the repression of natural sexual desires, the question should be asked whether acquisitivity is as fundamentally a part of human nature as sexuality. Presuming that acquisitivity is an inherent characteristic of human nature, perhaps government and public policy should be as circumspect in inhibiting its free exercise as has been the case with sexual practices.

Stated another way, acquisitivity appears to deserve as vigorous advocacy in favor of its free exercise as Freud provided on behalf of sex and the libido. After all, the artificial repression of the desire to acquire certainly holds the latent potential for psychological dysfunction. And society stands to benefit considerably more from the free exercise of acquisitivity than from sexual profligacy.

Acquisitivity, by all indications, serves an essential function as the natural mechanism for free markets and ultimately the survival of mankind. If that is the case, its protection and encouragement by society are arguably as worthy goals as freely consensual sexual conduct consistent with procreation and familial relations.

The comparability of sex and acquisitivity in human nature is not the point at issue here. The point is that a reevaluation of views and policies affecting acquisitive practices of individuals from the viewpoint of society, especially by the intellectual community and by government, is entirely warranted.

The primary alternative to individual acquisitivity in private transactions as the mechanism for allocating resources has been collective decision-making through governmental institutions. The former Union of Soviet Socialist Republics used central planning of resource allocation, thereby providing practical evidence of the inferiority of such arrangements to the mechanism relied upon by free markets. One can scarcely question the strength of intellect or the educational support furnished by the USSR in its efforts to assure the success of its bureaucracies. Yet within 70 years the superiority of one mechanism over the other could no longer be denied.

Millions of minds motivated by self-interest make better decisions than a few minds, no matter how intellectually brilliant the few may be, when acting upon matters directly affecting those millions of individual human beings. The central planning of the USSR was so incapable of making sound decisions in allocating resources among the millions of its own people that its most lasting monument may be the image of Soviet institutions crumbling before cheering throngs of former subjects.

Central planning of resource allocation among the people is inferior to the mechanism of the market for accomplishing the task. This principle holds true in all forms of government, including republican democracies such as the United States of America. The policies of Western democracies ordinarily allow the market to function so that most private transactions occur largely as they otherwise would. However, the governments extract a portion of the value of each transaction through taxation, partly as a means of redirecting the market allocation of resources.

In the United States, reallocation of resources has been carried to such an extent as to be called "redistribution of the wealth" in recent years. This social policy expresses the objectives of winning the war on poverty, reducing disparity in income levels, and assuring a safety net of minimal subsistence for those persons unable to provide for themselves. Even the substantial resources directed for use in retirement of the elderly are in the nature of centrally planned transfers of resources from currently young, working people to others of more advanced years.

These may be worthy goals, but implementation of the underlying programs undeniably redirect the allocation of resources that would result solely from the private transactions of individuals. To that extent, the resulting allocations are the products of central planning. The systemic problems facing Social Security, Medicare and other such programs in the United States are indicative that central planning in democracies is not vastly more effective than in totalitarian communist governments.

The essential reason that central planning is ineffective is that central planners are individuals, too, and each individual customarily acts upon self-interest. The self-interest of a central planner, as with other individuals, involves providing for himself and his family, keeping his job, advancing his career and similar concerns. This may motivate him to try to do his central planning well, but it will not enable him to see and understand any better the self-interests of the millions of other individuals who will be affected by his central planning decisions.

Those millions of individuals can see and serve their own interests far better than the central planner, particularly when he cannot possibly know what those interests are. That is equally true in the USA as in the former USSR, and will remain so, albeit that republican democracy may produce somewhat greater responsiveness to and insight into the desires of the people.

There is at least a significant probability that humans were created, or have evolved, with an inherent nature designed to allocate resources among themselves in a manner that may best provide for the ultimate success and survival of the species. This circumstance gives pause to the notion that the proper role of government is to interdict or to manipulate that natural mechanism. The potentially cataclysmic effect of such interdiction or manipulation is, at a minimum, sufficient grounds to question the wisdom and reevaluate the policies of government that impinge upon the natural mechanism for allocation of scarce resources already in place.

Let us assume that, for purposes of debate, survival of the species is ultimately in very close balance. Let us assume further that the smallest deviation from the natural arrangement for efficient allocation of resources will certainly prove fatal for all humanity at a future date. Governmental demands for reallocation of resources are undoubtedly capable of so much mischief in interdicting the design of human nature that the chances for human survival will be materially and decisively diminished.

In the face of such dire consequences, the government's first duty should be comparable to the primary principle of the Hippocratic Oath undertaken by the medical profession: "first do no harm" in the policies and mandates imposed upon the governed. All governments should be open to careful reevaluation of laws affecting the acquisition and ownership of resources by their people.

Of course, the "natural arrangement" for allocation of resources includes voluntary reallocation of resources on moral and ethical grounds, since humans are naturally apt to act upon such humanitarian concerns. Fears that charitable care for those in need would be absent in such circumstances are, therefore, unfounded.

Reevaluation of existing views and policies towards acquisitivity by society is only the starting point. New challenges, as well as correcting mistakes repeated after unlearned lessons of history, must be addressed if we are to approach the potential for achieving the full benefits of acquisitivity as a naturally occurring resource in human nature.

The issue of dealing with genetic manipulation of the "acquisitivity gene" by individuals or by governments is only one of the more esoteric concerns, but certainly is no less profound in its moral and social implications than the similar issue relating to the "mothering gene." Aside from such futuristic concerns, however, a multitude of far-reaching and powerfully influential policies are already reflected in governmental and private institutions.

The designs of taxing statutes and social welfare benefits are among the many ways in which governments exert very strong pressures upon the acquisitive conduct of private individuals. The developing appetite of governments for so-called "asset forfeiture" laws, given footing in the United States in the "war against drugs," already has spread to some 300 federal statutes and innumerable state laws.

Such statutes take property purportedly as a means of fighting crime, but create serious conflicts of interest by allowing the taken property to be kept by the policing agencies. Government usurpation of private rights threatens to do substantial and widespread harm to the free exercise of acquisitivity. Indeed, as reflected in the Takings Clause of the Fifth Amendment of the U.S. Constitution, the Founding Fathers had a more refined understanding of acquisitivity, and a more fortified appreciation of the importance of the sanctity of property ownership in the acquisitive process, than do many public officials today.

The extent of social welfare reform that has occurred within the United States in recent years has already impinged somewhat upon the subject of how government programs can encourage rather than inhibit personal enterprise. A fledgling but potentially burgeoning debate has begun regarding federal tax policy, and whether primary reliance upon income taxes rather than a tax on consumption should be reconsidered and remedied. An improved understanding of acquisitivity as an element of human nature can be beneficial, and may be pivotal, in making such decisions that have helpful or harmful effects upon the daily lives of so many individual human beings.

Let us return for a moment to the hypothetical scenario previously posed in which the survival of humanity depends upon a swift frontrunner arriving at a crucial future juncture in time. The encouragement and nurturing of innovative frontrunners would seem to be a subject worth exploring further. What makes such a person function and what hinders the essential performance?

A person presently acknowledged to be one of the pivotal innovators of the technological revolution springing from the "silicon valley" area around San Jose, California, is Jim Clark. A recently published book[9] traces Clark's evolution from his expulsion as a high school junior from the public schools of Plainview, Texas, through his higher education in mathematics, physics and computer science.

Clark conceived the idea of using mathematics through software programming to enable computers to assist the graphic design of items such as cars and airplanes. Clark founded Silicon Graphics, Inc., to exploit this technology, but was soon removed from any position of real control and influence in the corporation allegedly due to his personal abrasiveness and unpredictability. Clark then conceptualized a new product called a telecomputer as a means of saving SGI from economic oblivion at the hands of Microsoft's competitive domination. However, after having the telecomputer project stripped of his influence by SGI, Clark finally left SGI in early 1994.

In leaving SGI, Clark was keenly aware that he and the other engineers who founded SGI had been largely excluded from great financial gain, and he was determined to see that such an experience did not recur in his next endeavors. Author Michael Lewis relates that money and power were among Clark's motivations in his search for what next to do,

> "But that version of events is misleadingly neat. Clark didn't conceptualize his new role: he groped for it. He had an animal desire to have what he wanted and not to have what he did not want. He wanted Silicon Valley to be even more suited than it already was to his talent

for anarchy. He wanted to harness the forces of creation and destruction. He did not want to manage a large company. He did not even want to be a venture capitalist.... He wanted to create *the* company that created the future. Once he had done that, he wanted to do it again and again and again and again. For his services he wanted to be treated better, and paid more, than anyone else."[10]

This is a vivid and indelible portraiture of acquisitivity in a frontrunner. The innate, burning desire to create the company that creates the future, and then to do it again repeatedly, may be the essence of what is needed by the frontrunner to win the hypothetical race for survival on behalf of mankind.

Perhaps the animal desire for control and the talent for anarchy likewise are essential ingredients in the mixture of fuel for the frontrunner. But most certainly the desire to be paid, the instinct to acquire, the acknowledgement that acquisitivity must attract resources commensurate with the creative contribution: this is an element both essential and inevitable in the formulation of a successful innovator. Essential because acquisitivity attains the resources required for motivation and for production. And inevitable because acquisitivity is so inherent in human nature.

The hypothetical scenario assuming mankind will perish unless certain minimal progress is achieved by an unknown future date certain is probably too simplistic. More likely, the challenge facing humanity is to achieve minimal progress on a multitude of fronts simultaneously and then to do it again and again and again. Such a challenge will require that every person perform as a frontrunner to the ultimate extent of his capabilities. Government will need to acknowledge this scenario and assure that enforced public policy does not get in the way.

Mounting evidence from the life sciences will likely prove in the foreseeable future what many have intuitively understood for centuries: that human nature includes a persistent desire, instinct or spirit to acquire. Human acquisitivity may be directed towards material goods, information, companionship or other matters of interest. As it affects all matters having value to the person, acquisitivity provides an extremely powerful mechanism for the efficient allocation of resources useful in the production of greater wealth.

This natural mechanism deserves much closer consideration and appropriate deference from society and government when economic policies would impinge upon its free and unfettered exercise. We have much to gain from greater understanding of acquisitivity, probably more than we can presently know and appreciate.

Two
Acquisitivity Examined

Adam Smith observed in humans "the propensity to truck, barter, and exchange one thing for another" and attributed to this characteristic the "necessary...consequence" that productive work be divided into specialties.[11] By means of such specialization, a worker could greatly increase efficiency and productivity, and thus personal income and wealth. Both specialization and trading might properly have been identified by Smith as tools designed to serve the more fundamental aspect of human nature that seeks the acquisition of property.

Education, training, specialization, trading—these are practices and methods, among many others, adopted and adapted by men and women as tools to aid in their quest to acquire. Throughout history, long past the time when Smith wrote, and presently, acquisitivity has been exercised by most of mankind on a scale designed to enable personal survival or improvement of living conditions. Many would describe their own efforts in this respect simply as "making a living." Those circumstances still exist today for the great majority of the human race.

But in Western societies, and even in Africa and Asia, the acquisitive process that is readily apparent in the conduct of many individuals goes so far beyond mere survival, so far beyond subsistence or making a living, that something more must be at the root of it. After all, if "making a living" is the best we can do to identify the human motivation involved, those individuals who work, produce and acquire far past the limits of necessity are likely to be viewed as engaging in aberrant behavior. Indeed, such an individual may be judged to be obsessed, to be going overboard with his work, and even to be "greedy;" that is, to be a bad person who ought to be deterred or even punished. Such an opinion about highly acquisitive people will produce public opinion that, over the long term, will discourage and deter to some degree the objectionable conduct.

But what if "making a living" is not really the basic instinct at all, but rather an economic necessity whose performance is enhanced by a more elemental aspect of human nature? Upon closer inspection, the human motivation may arise from a natural instinct to acquire property, with "property" defined in its broadest sense to include all things of value, whether material or inchoate.

The purpose to be served by this natural design should first be given a thoughtful evaluation. Then the conduct of those who acquire far beyond the bounds of their personal needs may be seen and evaluated in a different light. Illumination of natural acquisitivity may be critical in developing public encouragement of productive work by the most able among us. Presently the negative appraisal of wealth acquisition under existing mainstream perceptions so often apparent in society is undoubtedly influential in repressing acquisitive conduct.

The cause of conduct that amounts to making a living, and of the much broader acquisitive process in which a relatively elite few engage, may be identical in human nature. An improved understanding of the character and origin of this cause or motivational force is potentially very significant, both for public policy and for individual decision making.

Some societies or groups, for example, espouse cultural or political views that a person should not seek to acquire more property or wealth than is reasonably required for his or her family's needs. These views, and public policies derived from them, are connected with the supposition that more property or wealth acquired by one person necessarily means less property or wealth available for others. Economic competition is, so to speak, a "zero sum game" in which a gain for one person must result in an equal loss for another.

Of course, this superficial analysis has long since been disproved to the satisfaction of those exposed to elementary economic or market theory. But populist political rhetoric often ignores the greater wisdom that both parties in a market transaction ordinarily benefit relatively equally. Thus each party to some extent becomes at least somewhat wealthier, or else the transaction never occurs.

A more enlightened public discourse and policy might treat acquisitivity as a benefactor of society at least on the same par as productivity, creativity and innovation. Confronting the issue whether government should encourage or discourage acquisition of wealth beyond the personal needs of the individual, therefore, has far reaching and even pivotal consequences in today's post-modern society.

The employment laws of France prohibit any person within its jurisdiction from working more than 38 hours within a single week unless that employee is paid 150% of his customary wage, with violations punishable by criminal sanctions including fines and imprisonment. During 1998, government prosecutors charged several persons employed by the same company with criminal conduct consisting of intentional employment beyond the 38-hour limit. Such government policy and enforcement clearly has consequences for the individuals charged, but also for the society as a whole.

Consider the difficulty one person may have "making a living" within the 38-hour limit as compared to another person whose intelligence is higher, or who has inherited wealth. Is France providing a fairer or more just society than one that lets each person work to his own satisfaction with the talents at his disposal? Consider further the difficulty a French company will have in such circumstances when its executives, managers and workers cannot expend the efforts (at least not if more individual time is required) to compete with others in the world market who are not subjected to such restrictive employment laws.

At approximately the same time the French prosecutions mentioned above were proceeding in court, the European Union announced a new monetary unit known as the "Euro" to compete over the long term with the U.S. Dollar as the primary reserve currency to be used in international trade. Any national currency maintains its value, if at all, based upon the productivity and efficiency of the economic activity that supports it. Surely public officials ought not be surprised if the value of the Euro monetary unit falls in relation to a competing currency that is unfettered by such employment policies as those of France. If other European states make the same policy judgments as France, the prospects for the "Euro" becoming the dominant and preferred currency of the free market appear less than bright.

On a similar note, until recently the government of Germany imposed a tax equal to 50 per cent of the value of assets of a business corporation acquired by another such corporation. Obviously, such a tax expresses a strong public policy against such corporate acquisitions, while protecting corporate managements from takeover by others. In the year 2000, Germany repealed that confiscatory tax law, thus clearing the way for corporate restructuring in the European business community that may be critical to its success in world markets. This is an important example of government reducing its interdiction of market forces so that economic efficiencies may be achieved. Those efficiencies will improve the prospects of the Euro or whatever currency is used in the affected economy.

Public policy that undercuts the nation's currency is an equally serious undercutting of the personal well-being of its own people, as is clearly apparent to a person prohibited from working to improve his circumstances. At this late stage of post-modern society, public policy consisting of moral, ethical and even criminal principles derived from the view that the market is a zero sum game is irresponsible in the extreme.

Public policy should take note, as an increasing number of states in the world have in recent years, that society has a direct stake in the success of its most creative, innovative and productive (and thus its most acquisitive) members. This direct stake does not mean, however, that government should involve itself in determining who succeeds or who fails in private business ventures.

Left alone, some individuals will succeed while others will fail in attempting to create a productive enterprise that will profit by serving the needs of the market. Those who innovate most rapidly and creatively do so without need or wish for government assistance. Indeed, if left alone, the best of innovators will progress considerably faster than would be the case when government programs are in place to take a part of their resources for the use of those who would otherwise fail. Before accepting the conventional wisdom from across the political spectrum that the "compassionate" role of government is to assure that "no one is left behind," the potential significance of slowing the frontrunner should be weighed carefully for its impact upon the long range interests of society.

Perhaps no better example of the frontrunner unfettered by government barriers can be found than in the technological world of information and analysis known as the internet. The rapidity of change and innovation, first in the development of computer capabilities and then in communications, has been truly breathtaking. Such progress is inconceivable in any field already closely regulated by government.

Fortunately, the speed of development of the internet and related technologies was so great that government has so far been unable to find a means of controlling it. Or, perhaps government has been sufficiently insightful to decline to do so. Although the U.S. government significantly deferred progress in telecommunications for years based on thoughts of continued tight regulatory controls of the industry, the Telecommunications Act of 1996 finally introduced important new competitive opportunities. That is the direction public policy needs to take if the natural mechanism of acquisitivity is to be exercised more freely.

The ultimate fate of mankind, in terms of success or extinction as a species, may depend upon the rapidity or timing within which a particular idea or discovery is made. If that hypothesis is valid, theoretically only one person or organization needs to be swift enough to find the concept or achieve the goal on a timely basis. Since we know neither the concept nor the time constraints involved in the race, we must assume that the race is to be run by many individuals with many concepts, each acting concurrently and urgently.

In order to accomplish their missions, the ones racing ahead may require tremendous resources at their disposal. Of course, any particular endeavor of this nature may ultimately prove unsuccessful, and the resources expended may appear to be entirely wasted. That is the risk of the front-running explorer, who must somehow gather the resources necessary before the mission can be undertaken.

However, governments are presently actively involved in assuring that "no one is left behind" in the acquisition of wealth. To achieve this announced public objective, resources are redistributed through various legislative designs to those less able to lead the exploratory missions. The fundamental drawback of this approach is that discovery of the penultimate idea or breakthrough may be crucially delayed (or even prevented entirely) beyond the time of its pivotal utility. Thus, artificial redirection by government of resources contrary to allocations made by the natural mechanism of individual acquisitivity arguably may be more harmful than beneficial to society over the long term.

By this analysis, the public pursuit of egalitarian goals may prove to be counterproductive to the most fundamental interests of society as a whole. Stated another way, egalitarian goals may serve short term interests of the poor by improving comfort and consumption, but at the same time may be contrary to the long term interests of society as a whole, including the poor.

When the humanitarian concerns for short term survival have been satisfied, even the classes benefited by government egalitarianism would not likely choose comfort, consumption or improved productivity above the long term success of humans as a species. Therefore, public policy should be very reluctant to provide for redistribution of resources by government edict when the effect over the long term may be detrimental in the most significant way.

The role of government in improving the welfare of "those left behind" by economic progress is not the only question to be examined regarding public policy. Assuming acceptance of the hypothesis that the best innovators ought to have adequate resources to enable a race towards progress, should the government determine the goals of the race or who is allocated those resources? The lessons provided by the now defunct Soviet Union and by the economic stagnation experienced under other modern socialist governments teach that individuals acting freely in the market provide a superior alternative to government control.

On the other hand, other non-governmental institutions of society that do not have the power of law to enforce their policies should continue to be free to influence the conduct of individuals in their use of resources. Obviously, the personal views and choices of each person regarding the use of any accumulated resources ought to be the primary determinant of their deployment, whether for production or consumption. Those individual judgments should be made within the context of human concerns of every nature.

Certainly considerations of morality, ethics and traditional concepts of right and wrong play appropriate roles in such decisions. With that being the case, institutions of religion and education have the full opportunity to exert their persuasive influences over the disposition of resources available for use by each individual and organization. However, as shown by the lessons of history, such institutions as churches and universities should be limited to the powers of voluntary persuasion to obtain acceptance of their views and principles by each individual in the conduct of private affairs.

Consumption plays an equally fundamental role with acquisitivity and productivity as elements of the natural mechanism for allocation of resources among human beings. Consumption at its most basic level is the essential motivation for both acquisitivity and productivity. Consumption of necessities such as food, fuel, clothing, shelter, water and medicine is a matter of survival for each individual. Every person is born with the lifelong challenge to acquire these necessities for consumption or die.

More people today are born into circumstances in which the risk of loss of the bare necessities appears objectively to be quite negligible. Even to those few, the risk may seem very real. The reality, however, for the overwhelming majority of human beings is an entire lifetime within the realm of never-ending concern and, yes, struggle, for the resources necessary for personal consumption. That struggle and the need to satisfy consumptive requirements will continue throughout the indefinite future as the primary impetus behind the drive for acquisitivity and productivity for most people.

At the same time, the number of individuals living well above the level of bare necessity is growing at an increasing rate. How is consumption to be regarded in this circumstance? Public policy is often heard encouraging consumer spending as good for the national economy, without indications that consumption above the limits of bare necessity is to be avoided or abhorred. But is consumption in excess of necessity good, bad or indifferent?

That question, at least insofar as the moral issues are concerned, is best answered by each individual according to the moral principles applicable. Each person can decide whether consumption is a luxury and a use of resources that would be better directed either towards productivity or charity. The answer will undoubtedly vary in many circumstances and will be influenced by the views of religious and social institutions.

The economic role of consumption, nevertheless, will continue unabated, regardless of whether necessary or conspicuous. Consumption takes resources from the hands of persons willing to forego production and moves those resources to other hands potentially more willing to be productive.

The only useless resources are those that are idle. Yet truly idle resources are sometimes hard to identify. Consider gold, or diamonds, or furs suitable for use as clothing. For past centuries and currently, gold has been seen by some as an "investment." Gold may be an investment when owned by one who intends to add value by making jewelry, or dental aids, or similar industrial uses of gold as a commodity. But, in other instances, is gold really an investment or merely a means to hoard resources or to store wealth so as to avoid diminution in value caused by inflationary government conduct?

When the Disney character Donald Duck's Uncle Scrooge visited his vault room, he loved to sit among the stacks of money and the piles of gold coins, joyfully tossing them in the air. If such a vault could be found today, the resources piled within it could properly be viewed as idle in the sense that the wealth is not being currently used to create, to innovate or to produce. This realization may have been a central motivating factor behind the decisions of the Bank of England and other central banks of western governments during 1999 to begin selling reserves of gold held in such vaults for so many years.

Of course, even the purchase of gold serves the purpose of transferring resources to potentially productive hands. When Scrooge McDuck buys gold to store in his vault, the money he spends for the purchase goes to whoever is selling the gold, and ultimately to the miner and the mint that produced the coins. Thus, whether it is Uncle Scrooge buying gold or the lady next door buying diamond necklaces, furs and rings, the consumption transaction moves resources from the hands of the purchaser to hands potentially more focused upon innovation and production.

That is a fundamentally important contribution to the efficiency of the natural mechanism for allocation of resources to the most productive uses. As acquisitivity feeds productivity and consumption, consumption at all levels serves the useful purpose of moving resources from less productive to more productive hands.

In this comprehensive social context, then, the person confronts the responsibility to make each and every decision so as to accumulate and deploy resources to achieve the optimum productive result. Before applying principles of morality, ethics or religion to guide a particular decision, rationality requires that the person should first ascertain the facts to be considered. Those facts should include the necessities for food, clothing, shelter, health, recreation and the like.

Somewhere within the range between such facts of life and the guiding principles of conduct ought to be a place for consideration of the scientifically derived fact that humans have a natural desire to acquire property. Likewise, the person should give weight to the rational conclusion that this natural characteristic was intended as an inborn mechanism to allocate resources efficiently for purposes of greater productivity. With these elements in the mix of considerations affecting decisions, other influences upon the individual, both in his efforts to acquire property and in his use or expenditure of wealth accumulated, may well produce a different judgment and outcome than would otherwise be the case.

Realizing that acquisitivity is an intentional and critically positive element of human nature designed to increase productivity, a person will likely give even greater energy and attention to the question: How can I become more acquisitive and productive? In some circumstances, the answer may be more preparatory education. In others, the answer will be less consumption, leaving more resources to be invested back into the productive process. Or invested in research towards improvements in products or the production process.

Of course, these very concerns occupy much of the time and energy of productive enterprises already. However, from a moral and ethical viewpoint, the actions and processes involved in becoming more efficient are presently valued largely within the context of the pursuit of self-interest or, as otherwise known, the "profit motive." Presently much of the intellectual community treats the profit motive as merely a respectable reference to the sinful impulse called greed.

With greater understanding of the natural mechanism of acquisitivity, the profit motive should be seen as a good and useful vestige of the divinely natural design for human survival and success. The positive impact upon the mental, emotional and physical energies of each individual who crosses this intellectual Rubicon are potentially profound, as are the implications for improvements in personal conduct.

Adam Smith saw the human propensity to truck, trade or barter, coupled with the natural tendency to act in one's own self-interest, as giving rise to unintended, good consequences for society. These unintended consequences were produced as if through the work of an "invisible hand." The "hand," not the working individual, produced good for society as a whole. Or, perhaps more accurately, that is the manner in which Smith's writing has been understood and taught to others.

The economist-philosopher Michael Novak has pointed out that Smith used the "invisible hand" metaphor only once in the 903 pages of

An Inquiry into the Nature and the Cause of the Wealth of Nations on page 423 in a discussion of imports.[12] In describing the motivation of the individual in promoting domestic industry, Smith states:

"he intends only his own gain, and he is in this, as in many other cases, led by an invisible hand to promote an end which was no part of his intention."[13]

Smith may well have believed that particular individuals were motivated to do good for society. But his essential point was that such a beneficent motive is not a requisite ingredient to produce the resulting societal good from the self-interested efforts of individuals.

Upon further reflection regarding the aptness of the "invisible hand" metaphor, perhaps an equally or more apt interpretation of Smith's writing would be that the human propensity to engage with the market flows directly from the profit motive. The profit motive, in turn, stems from the natural, if not genetic, design of humans to acquire property. This acquisitive design itself is the natural mechanism for the efficient allocation within society of resources for production. Efficient allocation of resources according to the natural mechanism is key to human progress and survival.

Thus, the instrumentality for achieving societal good, indeed for achieving the vital interests of society, is not an "invisible hand" acting outside the realm of human intention or influence. Instead, the instrumentality is the human person, acting in accordance with a divinely inspired design laced into the very genetic makeup of each individual and all mankind by the Creator. Or, if you prefer, laced into the makeup of mankind by evolution of the species.

This seemingly minor distinction from the common modern interpretation of Smith's "invisible hand" metaphor is of no small consequence. The "invisible hand" does good for society without human involvement, or at least without human intent. By the "hand" analogy, the individual who toils in the market, if he is aware of the point at all, is told that he is greedily slaving solely in his own selfish interests. Yet, without his assistance or intent, the "hand" functions to make society better off. That scenario is both strained and off the mark, as is easily recognized when acquisitivity in human nature is taken into account.

The good of society flows directly from the individual as he exercises and exhorts the natural mechanism designed within his own character to allocate efficiently the resources needed for production. Particularly since motivation plays such a pivotal role in human performance, the individual should be informed of the benefits for society that flow from his personal efforts.

When a person works hard day by day, the solace, encouragement and invigoration to be realized from knowledge that the efforts exerted are viewed as beneficial to society rather than as entirely selfish are palpable. Multiply those benefits by the millions who seek a kind word for the dignity of their work and the potential rewards in human progress are staggering.

Improvement in state of mind or motivation of the worker is by no means the only way in which better understanding of acquisitivity in human nature can benefit society. Many public policies enforced by law cut across human activities that pursue the acquisitive and productive process. Americans often complain, and with reason, of the burdens placed upon them by their governments' taxes and regulations.

Yet immigrants continue to flock to the United States from countries across the world, primarily due to the relative freedom for economic productivity enjoyed in America as compared to their former homeland. Ironically, the concepts of liberty and freedom seem more abstract to Americans who have not lived in such foreign domains than to the immigrants who come to be free of very real and practical obstacles to their personal aspirations.

All governments, including the federal government of the United States, the constituent States and local authorities, engage to some degree in adoption of misguided policies inspired by majority or minority interest groups. Every public policy ought to be reexamined in light of a new understanding of human acquisitivity to assure that government meets the test: first, do no harm.

One of the perplexities of human success over past generations has been the propensity among offspring of so-called "self made" men to be less successful than their parents. "From rags to riches to rags again in three generations" has been a repeated lament regarding the difficulties experienced by children and grandchildren in their efforts to increase, or even to preserve, wealth accumulated by their successful progenitors.

A related aspect of this concern is the difficulty a parent raised in conditions of economic scarcity experiences while attempting to raise his own children in conditions of affluence.[14] A parent who experienced scarcity as a child understandably would concentrate his talent and energy upon the challenge to rid himself of the limits of that scarcity, and would want his own children to be free of such scarcity when affluence is at hand. By contrast, the child raised in affluence, even if purposely denied a surplus of material possessions, will grow to adulthood with an abundance of attention given to consumption, despite the best efforts of a parent attempting to teach industrious habits. By the time a second generation rises on such a foundation, finding grandchildren with personalities centered largely upon consumption, having little or no interest or talent for productivity, should not be surprising, although such an outcome is certainly not inevitable.

The essential lesson to be learned from these repetitive generational patterns is that the acquisitive mechanism works efficiently in both directions. Resources gained through its functioning are for use primarily in further productive activity, and are not to be directed towards consumptive excess. When a person focuses reasonably well upon productive work and is able to generate creative juices to guide personal conduct, success in acquiring additional resources can be realized beyond the limits of dreams. But, at the same time, if consumption is permitted by the individual to displace production as the focus of personal aspiration and as the purpose of acquired resources, that individual's resources will be depleted surprisingly promptly as they move into the acquiring hands of another more productive person.

This outcome is supported convincingly by data collected in social studies indicating a much higher incidence of upward and downward mobility among economic classes than is commonly believed. In other words, the acquisitive mechanism of human nature does not, in fact, provide unerringly for the rich to get richer and the poor to get poorer. On the contrary, studies show that often the case is that the poor get richer or the rich get poorer. Upon closer examination, these individual cases would evidence a high correlation to the effective employment of the acquisitive mechanism as the key factor in determining the particular outcomes.

When a poor person becomes rich, the pattern of conduct that has preceded this phenomenon is ordinarily a significant period of preparation through education, followed by a further significant period of work and creative productivity. Other factors such as windfall gains or inheritance may be present in particular cases, but creative and diligent productivity is overwhelmingly the most significant factor in producing wealth. Likewise, its diminution or absence is the primary causative factor when a person moves in the other direction from wealth towards poverty on the economic spectrum.

Factors such as increasing age, diminishing health and similar personal concerns may be contributing causes of the decrease in productivity. If the person who gains wealth, by whatever means, fails to use the additional resources in useful and productive ways, those resources will be depleted, sometimes sooner than imagined possible, and the person will return to relative poverty.

This outcome may occur even in cases where the assets have been acquired entirely through the efforts and productivity of the same person. However, having acquired the additional wealth, that person then changes his productive focus, perhaps due to the distraction or persuasion of consumptive pressures as a potential use of the newly acquired resources. Of course, such adverse outcomes often are not the case, because the experience of engaging in the acquisitive process is a good teacher.

Whether a person who gains wealth remains in that level of affluence, or becomes more or less wealthy, will depend primarily upon the same principles of the acquisitive process as applied before the wealth was first gained. The acquisitive mechanism provides the added resources so as to increase future productivity. So long as those resources continue to be put to efficient and productive uses, even greater resources will be added for the same purpose. But to the degree that efficiency and productivity are sacrificed to laziness, wasteful consumption or other such unproductive conduct, the store of resources will be affected and diminished accordingly.

The acquisitive mechanism shows no favoritism to a particular individual or to a particular group, neither to the rich nor to the poor. The mechanism operates continuously to move resources into the hands that will use them most efficiently, whether those hands belong to a person in America, in China, in Russia or in Africa.

True, a rich person has the present advantage of controlling existing resources that can be put to immediate use in a productive enterprise. That is, indeed, a significant advantage over a poor person whose ideas, energy and creativity could potentially put similar resources to prompt and productive use, yet must be accommodated to a slower accretion of resources. Nevertheless, the presently wealthy person is also challenged immediately by the acquisitive mechanism to put resources to productive use or lose them.

Thus, by one perspective, a person who begins in poverty benefits from the time and experience gained in acquiring property so that he can more successfully manage and deploy resources once they are gained. By comparison, the person beginning his working career with considerable wealth may find it lost through poor judgment before he learns what the acquisitive and productive processes demand.

Having placed a foot on the path towards improving productivity and making use of talents, a person may progress through multiple levels of concerns. The first step may be changing from a mental or physical condition of idleness into action, or from laziness to industriousness. Or a presently employed person may apply greater efforts towards production or towards advancement. These first elementary steps may prove to be pivotal and as fundamentally important as a breakthrough innovation achieved by a person at a more advanced stage of productive activity.

Each step must be seen, evaluated and initiated by the person involved in the making and implementation of his personal business plan. Whether that plan is concerned with creative arts or industrial manufacturing makes no difference so far as the necessity and function of the plan are concerned. Writing the essential structure of the plan may prove helpful in removing nebulous or ambiguous thinking, but planning for such purposes as improved productivity often is a continuous and never-ending process of change and adjustment. That process ordinarily involves a continuing series of decisions to be made regarding allocation of resources. At least when the person has clearly in mind a focus upon improving acquisitivity and productivity, the likelihood of success in making the right allocations is significantly greater.

Advancing along the path towards greater productivity can be a tremendously exciting and exhilarating experience. Those who have traveled the path for most of a lifetime often report that the journey itself, not the destination, provides the greatest joy and fulfillment.

Such an evaluation and outlook is entirely consistent with the manner in which acquisitivity operates in human nature. The exhilaration stems from actions that create, that innovate, so as to spur productivity and give rise to a successful response—usually in the form of greater accumulation of resources. But it is not the *having* of the greater wealth, or even the spending or consumption of it, that provides the most significant enjoyment to the person. Instead, the successful entrepreneur most often treasures the critical acts of productive decision-making as the "golden days" of a working lifetime. The common assessment that exhilaration and personal fulfillment flow from productive and creative conduct may rightly be seen as additional proof of the existence of natural acquisitivity in each human being.

Having said all this about the close and symbiotic relationship between acquisitivity and productivity, the essence of the motive for acquisitivity is not precisely productivity. Personal liberty is a better description of what makes acquisitivity function in human nature. A person aspires to acquire property in order to exercise the freedom to decide how to enjoy the property once acquired. The enjoyment may, indeed, be expressed through greater productivity. If that choice is selected through the individual's expression of discretion, then the greater productivity will bring additional resources. Those added resources will likewise be subject to the exercise of personal liberty to make the choices of potential uses for them.

Consumption is one of those potential uses, which may range from basic necessities to lavish high living. In any form of consumption, its cost effectively moves resources from the consumer to hands that are potentially productive.

Charity is another potential use of resources. Ordinarily a charitable use of resources would be spent relatively promptly for consumption of necessities by the beneficiaries. Gifts to charitable trusts, however, are often invested for productive purposes, with only the earnings from such investments being expended directly for charitable beneficiaries.

But it is the human aspiration for this full range of discretion in satisfying needs and desires of various kinds that fuels acquisitivity in human nature. In the human experience, a variety of choices for use of resources may be right or wrong in the specific circumstances of the individual. Life involves a broad scope of concerns, only some of which are economic. The economic reality remains, however, that use of resources to improve productivity, particularly in creative and innovative ways, will provide additional resources to the person who makes that choice.

This is merely a meager, initial effort to give acquisitivity the attention and understanding it deserves. The efforts, analyses, opinions and criticisms of many others will be required to advance understanding of this crucially important subject to the level of enlightenment we should have reached long ago.

Three
The Enlightenment

What a time to be alive and awake to the enlightenment that acquisitivity is more about production than about consumption! After centuries of human struggle to eke out a bare living from the resources of nature or from the hand of others better off, history has arrived at a time with a clearer view of what the acquisitive nature of humans was designed to accomplish.

This inherent spark in men and women was not intended merely to enable a person to crawl from the mud onto a plane of relative comfort and dignity, but to go no farther. Neither was bare necessity to be the line of demarcation beyond which only the sinfully greedy would venture. No, the characteristic that so distinctively marks the intellect, the emotions and the conduct of men and women has a more lofty and esoteric role than this, albeit that daily sustenance is a most fundamental and continuing concern for most of humankind even today.

The acquisitive spirit woven into the natural fabric of each person is the engine that propels the individual and society past the point of survival, not with survival as the ultimate goal line but as the starting place.

And the propulsion then continues onward towards ultimate success as a species.

The power of this engine has already begun to be recognized as societies across the world allow incrementally more leeway for each individual to conceive and reach for better possibilities in his own life. Yes, the acquisitivity engine that drives creativity, innovation and production has achieved ignition and liftoff. But the progress to date may be relatively modest when compared to the journey ahead.

Still, the tools already fashioned and placed at our disposal are so potent as to be breathtaking. The stored knowledge and reserved capital available for productive ends in 1999 are so vast that mere rationality provides no logical point to begin or end an inventory. As a token effort towards the assessment of these riches, for example, one might consider a topic not ordinarily associated immediately with productivity or economic survival: music.

Only a few thousand years ago, human experience was almost entirely barren of music. Between then and now, human talent and understanding required for creating, performing and recording music has expanded almost beyond comprehension. Composition of music through use of standardized scales and notations, design and production of instrumentation of every variety, the cultivation of human skills in the use of instruments, electronic amplification and recording, and wireless and internet communication of music. This is no more than a cursory listing of the various fields in which almost unimaginable strides have been made to create and establish a virtual free public library of rich musical resources.

Today each person can be a patron of that free musical library that allows unlimited access to priceless assets no one of us could hope to replicate anew in a lifetime devoted to the task. A "free library card," as it were, allows each person living today to experience and enjoy the musical wealth built over the centuries by our predecessors. This is a benefit and resource with value beyond estimation.

Musical wealth is, in many of its aspects, shared at least to some degree by all. And the measure of this store of wealth has been and is being increased incrementally year by year and day by day. The point can hardly be contested that any person born today awakes to more wealth in musical resources alone than any king's ransom could have purchased a mere 300 years ago.

Much the same case can be made for the wealth created and stored in innumerable other fields. Consider chemistry, physics, agriculture, law, medicine, philosophy, transportation, government, nutrition, communications, electronics, computers, architecture, construction and mathematics. The list goes on so long as to seem endless.

Each field provides wealth of great value for acquisition and use by every person in his own quest, whatever that quest may be. This wealth may be extracted and acquired in many significant ways regardless of the proprietary ownership of a particular idea, and regardless of how much wealth may have already been realized through proprietary rights by the person or entity who created the resource originally.

For example, consider the field of government. Those who lived in the American colonies in the Eighteenth Century devoted much of their time and energy, and in many cases sacrificed their lives, in the arduous task of achieving a constitutional structure for government. Their more specific goal was to create restraints on government powers through constitutional limits to protect the rights of individuals. Since the government under consideration was intended to be a republican democracy, their particular concerns were to protect against excessive government actions motivated by either majoritarian or factional pressures. George Washington, John Adams, Benjamin Franklin, James Madison, Thomas Jefferson, Thomas Paine and many others necessarily expended very considerable portions of their lives and fortunes to establish that institutional structure for governance.

The resulting Constitution of the United States of America and amending Bill of Rights provided a foundation for personal progress and betterment that is immeasurable in value to each and every person living under its protections. In the most practical sense, the constitutional rights of each American citizen (and each person residing within U.S. borders) are wealth-producing assets of the highest importance. Without those hard won gains achieved through the contributions and sacrifices of previous generations, each American would begin life much, much poorer in his prospects for improving his circumstances.

The same can be said about the infrastructure of laws and judicial administration established to resolve disputes, punish criminal conduct and expedite commerce. The slightest reflection upon the presently severe shortcomings of Russia in the realm of such legal arrangements ought to be persuasive as to their value to private citizens pursuing self-interest. A person required to fend for himself in a lawless jungle will promptly adjudge his circumstances to be at a great commercial disadvantage in comparison to an individual who does business in a society well ordered for commerce. More people in countries around the world during the late Twentieth Century are finding greater economic freedoms and improved legal infrastructures to be invaluable resources as they embark upon creative and productive enterprises.

The advances of medicine are available to aid a person's effort to maintain the health of himself and his family relatively conveniently and at manageable cost. Compare that circumstance with a person living 100 or even 50 years ago and you will conclude that medical resources provide valuable foundational and operating support for a person engaging in acquisitive activity today. In every field examined, the accumulation of knowledge available for creative and productive use by any person, or available to liberate that person to pursue his own passions in any other field, are assets of incalculable worth.

One of the most far-reaching and beneficial innovations to spring from the business and legal fields is the corporate design for assembling and managing capital to be used in production. Acquisitivity disbursed among six billion individuals is a productive and innovative engine with tremendous diversity. Nevertheless, if the extent of accumulated capital were to be limited to the success of an individual in acquiring resources within his or her own lifetime, or even within succeeding generations of the same family, the possibilities for undertaking larger business ventures would be quite confined.

The Industrial Revolution was importantly aided by the use of the business corporation legal structure. The corporation enabled innovative individuals to assemble capital from others to support productive business plans. Governments of industrialized countries have adopted laws to expedite the formation and operation of corporations, and to expedite investment of capital in their securities. Securities exchanges and other formalized arrangements for trading securities of corporations now provide an efficient and broadly used mechanism for channeling capital to its most productive uses.

The institutions that enable the leveraging of individual acquisitive conduct so that capital can be assembled much more quickly to implement innovative ideas were established through years of effort and experience. They now constitute assets of great value available for use by each individual in furthering acquisitive and productive goals.

Consider the phenomenon of a group of middle-aged women in a small town of the United States coming to national public attention through their success as an investment club. Such an occurrence is possible only through the institutional infrastructure of corporate securities and the markets for buying and selling shares of stock. These market mechanisms enable the women involved to improve their own financial well-being through careful investment. At least equally important, however, is the function served by these women and the same mechanism in bringing additional capital into productive use.

Imagine the effects on economic productivity if corporate securities and the markets for trading them did not exist. The capital owned by the women of the small town could only be deposited in a bank or savings account, or invested in business enterprises operated by the individual or by business associates. The loss of efficiency in the productive use of capital would be devastating, not only to the women as individuals but also to the potentially burgeoning business enterprises starved of the use of their capital. Multiply this stifling effect upon the efficient deployment of capital by applying the same limitations to every individual, small town and metropolis around the world and the monumental importance of free market capitalism can be appreciated more fully.

Turned around to the positive view of the circumstances we presently behold, the securities markets are treasures of the greatest significance to every person, regardless of whether that individual actually makes a direct investment in a corporate security. And the financial markets are even a greater treasure if a person prepares and enables himself to make capable use of them.

On November 5, 1913, the world acclaimed engineer William Mulholland opened the giant sluice gates of the just-completed aqueduct bringing water from the Owens Valley of the Sierra Nevada Mountains to the future metropolis of Los Angeles.

"At first the crowd saw only a trickle, which suddenly became a stream and then a raging torrent as it flowed in the culvert below them. From high in the snow pack of the Sierra Nevada 233 miles north all the way to the San Fernando Valley, eight thousand miner's inches were pouring from the hatches and splashing down the chutes in a veil of spray above newly man-made falls. ...And almost in a flash of an eye, there was delivered to the people of Los Angeles an asset worth a hundred million dollars—four times the cost of the aqueduct. It brought assurance of metropolitan grandeur and future prosperity such as few cities of the world can hope to attain."[15]

Pointing to the sparkling water bursting through the opening gates and spilling into the dry environs of southern California, Mulholland implored the assembled crowd of 43,000 dignitaries and common citizens: "There it is! Take it!"[16]

The water brought to Los Angeles by an engineering feat of historic dimensions, at the time second only to the Panama Canal in its magnitude, is commonly acknowledged to have given birth to productive and innovative activity of equally historic proportions.

Today, behold and contemplate the prodigious reservoirs of stored knowledge, constructed infrastructures both physical and intellectual, and technologies of every description available to serve the needs and desires of humans! Mulholland today could point to these resources and again exhort with even greater conviction: *"There it is! Take it!"*

A person beginning his economic voyage today does not have to conceive, invent and implement the world wide web or the internet. Those monumental advancements are already in place, being improved at warp speed by many interested others, and ready for use by *you* to advance your own purposes. True, others accomplished those innovations, and undoubtedly many have grown much wealthier for having done so. But the point remains that the capabilities of those innovations exist and may be put to use for *your* own profit and according to *your* own vision. Before the internet existed, you had no such option. Your ends would have had to be achieved by other less expeditious means.

Obviously, the internet and a multitude of comparable innovations thus are significant assets available for use in building the resources of each individual. In this very real sense, every penniless person has immense wealth at his disposal for deployment in his own acquisitive efforts.

Each generation owes debts of gratitude to parents who saw that their children had a better home, better clothes and a better education, if possible, than they themselves had. Each of us stands on the shoulders of our mother and father, as they wish, so that we may reach higher and farther than they could. This has been the essential role of the family in social progress throughout history.

But this picture is incomplete unless we recognize that our point of beginning is also elevated by the contributions of all who have gone before us. Many, many lives never seen or touched directly will affect our own lives immensely for the better through their gifts to the reservoirs of knowledge and other wealth of every nature passed down to us.

The concern is often expressed that children born in the United States of America today are unfairly burdened with a heavy debt created by deficit spending by the government. In 1999, the total federal debt is reported to be between Five Trillion Dollars and Seventeen Trillion Dollars, depending upon whether so-called unfunded liabilities to government retirement plans are counted. Understanding that a trillion is 1,000 billion, and a billion is 1,000 million, each of the 285 million American citizens is estimated to owe more than $17,500 as a pro rata portion of the total debt.

Every citizen will not ultimately pay that amount, of course. The federal tax code is designed to collect a significantly higher portion of taxes from higher income taxpayers than from those in the middle and lower incomes, thus leaving some citizens with a considerably lower portion or none of the debt, and some much higher. This federal debt is almost never discussed by political leaders without lamenting about the unfairness of passing such a debt along to our children, who will have its burden without its benefits.

At least two things ought to be said about the federal debt that hardly ever are. First, the government should never spend funds taken by the power of taxation unless the expenditure is both wise and necessary in the public interest. If those tests are met, then the expenditure must be made, even if a deficit results. Neither the creation nor the elimination of a deficit is reason enough to make or to avoid the expense that is both wise and necessary.

The fact that the United States government has, in fact, an accumulated deficit attests only to the political decisions to spend, not to the wisdom or necessity of debts incurred. Those questions can be left for another debate, which would bear upon the issue of whether any portion of the existing deficit is "unfairly" imposed upon future generations.

The second point to be made is that the stated deficit of the U.S. government is ordinarily expressed only in terms of debts owed, without the accompanying information customarily included in the balance sheet and financial statements of any business. Namely, the accounting of assets owned by the government.

Without a responsible and accurate accounting of assets, no determination can be made of whether the assets exceed the liabilities, and thus whether a net worth or net deficit exists. Unless a reasonable accounting of the value of assets is fairly presented in the financial statements of the federal government, the description of the deficit and its significance is impossible to understand in proper context.

"Assets?", you ask. "Does the government have assets?" Well, of course, every person with any awareness of government operations well knows that the U.S. government has a great many assets. What are they, and what is their fair value? The answers to those questions are not a part of public discourse on the often-discussed subject of the federal deficit.

The government owns much land, the national parks and much more throughout the country, and the buildings in which federal business is conducted. Indeed, an entire federal agency, the General Services Administration, operates to administer and maintain such property, and to dispose of it and to acquire more property. The land underneath the federal highway system has been acquired at great expense, and its present market value is undoubtedly much higher presently than when acquired. Surely all of that property is capable of identification with a reasonably accurate statement of fair value.

The federal government demands no less of every citizen and business entity every year in the reporting and payment of income taxes. The federal government owns the instruments and weapons of national defense, which can be inventoried and valued, including the bases from which our military operates. The superhighways, bridges, waterways and other infrastructure for transportation and communications owned by the government, including the land acquired with tax dollars by the powers of eminent domain, ought to be reflected on a federal balance sheet.

When the financial picture of the federal government is completed and presented in full detail according to the practices of business accounting (allowing some discretion for protection of national security interests), any remaining concern for the federal deficit will be understood in a more complete context. If, by chance, the federal balance sheet shows that federal assets fairly valued exceed the reported deficit by any significant amount, or any amount at all, then the concern for unfairness of the deficit to future generations will be seen in a different light.

Suppose the value of federal assets exceeds Fifty Trillion Dollars. In that case, if assets worth Fifty Trillion are to be passed along to future generations, do morality and ethics require that those assets be completely free of any mortgage? Perhaps not, at least if paying off the mortgage completely in advance would bankrupt the present generation or significantly reduce the resources available to it for economic productivity. In any event, a fair reporting of the value of government assets ought to become a part of the public knowledge and discourse about the government deficit. Otherwise, deficit spending and its relation to the young and to future generations will not be understood.

In a broader context, however, the wealth and resources available to serve and benefit every person far, far exceeds the value of all assets that could properly be listed in the financial statements of any government. As previously discussed, those assets include the music, the literature, the mathematics, the medicine, the law, the governmental and private institutions, the communications and transportation facilities, all of the private businesses organized to serve your needs at the most competitive price—the list could go on and on.

These are resources to be marshaled to achieve a person's self-interest, and rightly can be appraised for value and included among the assets passed along to the young at no cost. With that accounting complete, we would likely find that each newborn today is considerably richer than those in any previous generation.

The point to be made, however, about the reason for exhilaration concerning the prospects for personal and societal advancement today is somewhat different from merely pointing to the value of accumulated knowledge and wealth. Perhaps this is a pertinent occasion to refer to the synergy of technology and ideas that has recently come into play.

To say that the internet represents faster and cheaper communications is true, but that does not say enough. The advances in technology already accomplished to support the more efficient functioning of the internet go far beyond merely allowing individuals to speak with each other more easily. The internet technology already in hand enables the communication of written expression of complex ideas and data, not simply vocal conversations. This means that the stored reservoirs of knowledge created by previous and current productivity are much more readily accessible to each person for use in his own endeavors. Now every person with access to a personal computer can mine the storehouses of information, ideas and data on a daily basis with an ease completely unparalleled in human history.

This synergy between the technology of the internet and accumulated wealth of knowledge makes that accumulated wealth exponentially more valuable than ever before to those who need to make use of it. The presently latent prospects of this synergy for speeding the advancement of individuals and society are likely to be historic in the proportions of their eventual effects.

The golden opportunity and the challenge presented to each person in today's world are to marshal these tremendously abundant resources for productive purposes. True, neither the buffalo nor the redwood is as abundant as once was the case. These facts are sad evidence of nature's

vulnerability to the depletion of earth's resources by human development. But the vast storehouses of resources in the forms of knowledge,
institutions and material assets of many varieties offset those depletions
many times over.

This is so manifestly true that no serious observer would contend
that mankind would be better served by returning to the conditions
existing in the world 200 years ago. The wealth of nations has grown
astoundingly since Adam Smith published in 1776. In some instances
that wealth has shown signs of almost exponential growth, as improved
conditions of individual liberty have permitted increased success in fulfillment of personal aspirations.

Indeed it is true that much of this wealth is privately owned, having
been created and acquired through personal endeavors. Thanks to
acquisitivity in human nature, those privately owned resources will feed
greater productivity and progress for society or the natural mechanism
will move the resources to more efficient hands. However, the additional point that must not be missed is that much of the valuable
resources produced by civilization is freely available for advancing the
self-interests of each individual.

In other words, by no means is all the "gold" in California in a bank
in the middle of Beverly Hills in somebody else's name. A great deal that
is golden in terms of its intrinsic value for wealth creation has been and
is being created in the corporate empires of Silicon Valley and Bellevue,
Washington. And much of value in these creations becomes quickly
available to all who can make use of it, sometimes at a price permitted
by the market and many times entirely free of charge. All that is
required is for a person to plug into the information channels, learn
about what is available and its capabilities, and then marshal those
capabilities to serve needs that are yet unmet.

By matching personal knowledge of unmet needs with new
capabilities for serving them in innovative ways, today's industrious
person will find productive opportunities for the deployment of

resources and capital. This is the acquisitive mechanism of human nature at work, being exercised and fulfilled. Its tremendously beneficial role for society as well as for the individual is easily recognizable over the past centuries.

The powerful role of acquisitivity in the explosively innovative development of internet technology is even more apparent currently as ideas and creativity race ahead, free of government regulatory barriers. Both the benefits and the visibility of the acquisitive mechanism ought to increase immensely as it becomes better understood by people and accommodated by governments on broader fronts.

Four

The Corporate Extension

The evolution of the modern business corporation has extended the acquisitive and productive capacities of individuals by enormous lengths. Until the advent of the corporation, the resources available to an individual for purposes of undertaking a productive enterprise were limited to the assets owned by him or by persons with whom he joined directly.

Unless the individual venturer were already wealthy, or was joined by a king (or queen, such as occurred in the case of Christopher Columbus), innovative (and therefore risky) ventures requiring investment of substantial resources were rarely undertaken. Neither was it common for an enterprise to extend beyond the lifetime of the organizing genius at its helm until the corporation provided the mechanism for achieving the significant business objective of perpetual existence.

In simplest terms, the corporation is a tool designed for use by one or more individuals to exercise acquisitivity. The desirability and even the necessity of such a tool became evident over early years of experience by the bourgeoisie and craftsmen of Europe. From the time the individual became imbued with the right to apply talents for acquiring assets, the prospect for joining together with others in a common enterprise produced both benefits and competing interests.

The person with a business plan and productive expertise desired a means of bringing additional resources into an enterprise in order to pursue his goals more rapidly, but without giving others control of the enterprise. The founding entrepreneur commonly viewed personal control as necessary to assure individual success as well as the success of the enterprise.

Concurrently, any other person contributing resources to the common enterprise had other independent interests to advance if invested resources were to be protected and enhanced. An investor will not have joint control over the manner in which the common enterprise is to be conducted. For that reason, the investor will want to be sure that the investment does not give rise to personal liability for the debts or wrongdoing of the common enterprise. Thus, the concepts of management control and limited liability of investors were born.

The design of the modern business corporation resolves a multitude of organizational concerns that commonly arise when capital resources are to be assembled and deployed in a common enterprise. The life of the corporation is perpetual, so that the death of an individual or a predetermined interval does not limit its operations. Management has direct control of the execution of the business plan of the corporation, but is subject to supervision and removal by a board of directors. The directors, in turn, are elected by the investors or shareholders of the corporation. The shareholders provide the equity capital for the business operations, but have no direct responsibility or liability for the conduct of business.

Organizational documents such as articles of incorporation and bylaws establish the procedural rights and duties of the investors, the directors and management to facilitate the business operations. And, last but not least, ownership of shares in the corporation may be conveyed from one investor to another when the existing shareholder wishes to discontinue his investment and recover his capital, presuming a willing buyer and a mutually agreeable price can be negotiated.

Recognizing the importance of the corporate enterprise in the business community, governments have enacted extensive statutory law that serves as legal infrastructure to facilitate the use of corporations to conduct business. In the United States, the State of Delaware has long held a preeminent position as the favored domicile of major business corporations. This has been the case largely because Delaware saw very early the opportunity to attract the corporate chartering activities (and related taxes) of large business enterprises. Delaware has done so by adopting statutory laws favorable to corporate promoters and management, who commonly select the state in which the corporation is to be organized.

Other states have attempted to follow Delaware's example with varying degrees of success, sometimes producing statutes that reflect competing interests other than management in the legislative process. Now, all state governments as well as foreign countries have statutory laws that facilitate the organization of business corporations.

Each state also requires the registration of foreign corporations in order to do business within the jurisdiction. While each government places some additional measure of regulatory burden upon the corporation, the net effect is that the corporation is the organization of choice for the largest business enterprises in the world today.

The essential reason this remains the case is the efficiency of the corporation in serving the competing interests involved in assembling and deploying capital resources for productive purposes. Again, the efficiency of the corporation in assembling capital is greatly facilitated by institutionalized arrangements for the purchase and sale of corporate shares. These arrangements are most notably reflected in the governmental regulation of stock exchanges and similar approaches to the purchase and sale of corporate shares of stock.

The primary public policy espoused through securities regulation has been the promotion of investment through the requirement of full, truthful and timely disclosure of information relevant to the business operations of the corporation whose stock is being traded. Full disclosure implemented with the aid of transparent accounting practices is viewed as the essential ingredient if investment in corporate shares is to be accepted as fair and inviting. By and large, to the extent this reasonably enlightened policy has been implemented in the various economic locales, markets in which capital can be raised efficiently have flourished.

The result is a multitude of capital markets around the world that have cultivated varying degrees of trust and confidence among participating investors. These investors regularly and often invest their capital resources under circumstances they perceive to entail acceptable risks and rewards.

Even American investors, or perhaps especially American investors, are finding with greater frequency acceptable opportunities to invest their capital in the corporate businesses organized in "emerging markets" of other parts of the world. Depending upon ever changing business and financial conditions, the securities markets in corporate stocks and fixed income bonds attract significant flows of capital from all parts of the world to New York, London, Tokyo, Hong Kong, Frankfort and other business centers.

The connection between the stock exchanges for trading in ownership of corporate shares and the characteristic of human nature that can be called acquisitivity is really quite remarkable, if not immediately apparent. The premise has already been advanced that the acquisitive nature of humans serves as a natural mechanism to allocate resources for their most productive use. The reach of that mechanism has been limited during most of the millennia of human existence to the capability of individuals to apply resources by their direct efforts. During the past 200 years, and particularly the last 100 years, the public markets for corporate stock trading have extended enormously the capability of each individual to deploy resources under his ownership.

The stock exchanges and securities regulations have provided the basic infrastructure to accomplish this feat. But the more recent revolutions in computer technology and communication have steeply increased the efficiency and reduced the costs of obtaining investment information. As the Twentieth Century closes, a larger proportion of the capital resources of the world is becoming available for relatively efficient investment in productive enterprises through corporate securities.

Much of the major media discussion of this phenomenon treats the widespread participation by individuals in stock investments as speculation at best and ill-advised gambling spurred by rank greed at worst. Yet, in terms of the relative success of investments, individuals investing in corporate stocks have historically acted quite conservatively and have often fared better than market averages or investment professionals. Indeed, many individuals actually invest by combining their resources in mutual funds that are managed by the professionals.

Warnings against speculation and admonishments against sinful greed are often beneficial in many circumstances. But the media's criticism of stock market popularity seems to be primarily a carryover of the same criticisms directed throughout the years by demagogic politicians against successful individuals who have acquired wealth through business acumen. Much of the mainstream media continue to miss what may have considerably greater significance—the astounding success of the securities markets in reducing the amount of earned capital wealth that is left idle or underutilized.

Much of the idle capital in the world has belonged to the hardworking individuals who acquire resources through lifetimes of effort and must shepherd those assets conservatively to avoid waste or loss. For ages such capital was stored in the form of precious metals, perhaps as "buried treasure" or under a mattress, or eventually in a bank or savings account. The economic implications of "digging up" that treasure and investing it in economic enterprises that create productive jobs anywhere in the world are staggering.

The prospects for this productive activity are carried into more homes each year by the newspaper, the telephone, the television, the personal computer and now by the internet and the world wide web. The added fuel for economic growth furnished by these improved communications contains the potential of historical consequences for human progress.

Five

Greed, Pride And Charity

Adam Smith's observation of the propensity of people to truck, barter and exchange one thing for another was made benignly, without attribution of a clear reason for the conduct. However, Smith suggested that this propensity was probably the consequence of "the faculties of reason and speech" rather than "one of those original principles in human nature."[17] Smith's purpose was to inquire into the effects of the conduct, not its cause or source.

Much the same can be said of others who have been inspired by Smith's teachings and have extended his work to the present extent of economic understanding. Intellectual interest and inquiry today remain focused upon the wherefore, rather than the why, of human commercial activity.

The capabilities of individuals participating in what has become known as the free market, or free enterprise, or market capitalism, to produce new wealth and thereby to raise measurably the living standards of whole populations are so clearly proven as to be largely unchallenged. The successes and benefits of individual acquisitivity are well established.

The time has long since arrived when more attention ought to be directed to the nature of the impetus for acquisitivity as an apparently universal human activity. Better understanding of the nature and origin of acquisitivity may help to overcome some of the obstacles that are raised by public institutions against its free exercise.

The protagonist of Wall Street investment capitalism in *The Bonfire of the Vanities*[18] asserts, implicitly in the book and expressly in the motion picture version of the very popular novel, the essential premise: "Greed is good." In support of this conclusion, the protagonist bond trader as "Master of the Universe" marshals arguments in the best tradition of the robber barons of Nineteenth Century mercantilism. Capital resources must be preserved and deployed in the most efficient ways possible in order to compete in the marketplace. Only in that way will jobs be created and maintained to the greatest extent possible for the working people. And the person who is able to envision and control the process of efficient deployment of capital is entitled to quench his greedy lust for money and power by laying claim to all of the wealth he can extract from the process as the spoils of battle.

Yet these arguments ring hollow. Why? We should not be surprised. Of course the arguments seem artificial and self-serving. They seem so because they argue the validity of a premise that is false and that we know to be false.

We know that *greed is not good*. We know that greed is actually selfish, immoral conduct and, according to Judeo-Christian teaching, is a sin. Therefore, by constructing as he does the premise to be argued in *The Bonfire of the Vanities,* the author creates an impossible task doomed to failure in its proffered defense of the capitalist ethic.

The flaws in the *Bonfire* debate, however, are not so much in the arguments presented in support of the premise as in the falsity of the assumption that underlies the premise itself. Asserting that "greed is good" as the principal line of defense for free market conduct presumes, or concedes, that greed is, in fact, the motive of those who engage in commerce.

"Greed is good" is a false premise erected upon a fallacious assumption; *i.e.,* that greed is the motive for business and commerce. Thus, by constructing its central premise to create a strawman rather than the most formidable principle available, *Bonfire* puts the capitalist at a considerable disadvantage. The resulting examination of the subject is much less interesting than might have been presented.

If greed is conceded to be the cornerstone of capitalism, the outcome of the debate is predetermined. Greed is commonly and correctly understood to be indefensible. A more compelling test of ideas flows from the clash of the optimum positions available to each of the competing propositions.

Closer examination of the nature of acquisitive conduct in commerce and business reveals the potential for much more defensible motivations than greed. Individuals act for a myriad of reasons in different circumstances, and sometimes with multiple motives even in a single instance.

Greed is commonly understood to be a voracious desire for money, wealth or anything of value to be used selfishly or in a miserly way. Doubtless, certain individuals may act regularly out of greed, and every person may experience greed on occasion.

However, greed simply cannot be attributed in a wholesale fashion to every person who awakes in the morning and has hopes and aspirations of being better off before he sleeps again. If this is true, therefore, the premise that "greed motivates acquisitive conduct" must contain a very large exception for ordinary working people who spend much of their lives and energies trying to advance the economic interests of themselves and their families.

In *Major Barbara,* the George Bernard Shaw epic play first published in 1913, the daughter of a super-rich armaments manufacturer becomes a devoted officer of the Salvation Army. Barbara would almost certainly concede that a person who works hard to earn money and gives a generous portion of it to the church or to charity can scarcely be accused of greed in pursuing such work.

That being the case, it seems wholly defensible from a moral viewpoint to assert that the wife and children of a working man are worthy of no less devotion and sacrifice on his part than public charity or the church. And, if the betterment of one's own family is socially desirable and to be encouraged as a matter of morality and public policy, acquisitivity for that purpose must be entirely appropriate.

When the ordinary working person passes moral muster for daily toil, each person (even the Wall Street investor or the Main Street businessman) is entitled to the same examination of motives before being condemned by a conclusion that greed is his principal motivator. One can hardly imagine a view objecting to the need for at least a fair examination of individual cases. Yet the public discourse rarely deals with the subject of investment, for example, without presuming that the motive for every investor is greed. At least that is the case in almost any political context, when such subjects as taxation and regulation of investors are on the table.

We may stipulate that greed is to be abhorred, and each person should strive to expunge it from his or her own character. "Selfishness has never been admired," wrote C. S. Lewis, the Oxford philosopher and prolific Christian author, in discussing "The Law of Human Nature." Lewis first expressed his observation in a series of radio addresses during the German bombardment of Great Britain in World War II, which were later published as a part of *Mere Christianity.* That selfishness has never been admired is certainly true.

But as much as human nature despises selfishness, at the same time human nature aspires to be acquisitive. Is this really a direct contradiction in human nature? Or is it hypocritical conduct? Perhaps either, but probably neither. If a characteristic such as abhorrence of selfishness is a part of human nature, then human nature is unlikely to contain the opposite characteristic at the same time.

Yes, by the power of independent thought and deed, a person may choose to act in a selfish way. But in so doing, the person will know of the wrongful conduct and will consciously or subconsciously abhor it in himself, and maybe even more sharply than he abhors it in others.

Is acquisitivity akin to selfishness as a type of abhorrent conduct that ought to be expunged from a person's character by his reasoned thoughts and deeds? Or is acquisitivity itself a part of human nature as is the abhorrence of selfishness? The weight of evidence seems to favor the conclusion that humans are acquisitive by nature.

If, for example, acquisitivity were to be expunged entirely from the human character (as selfishness should be), human beings could hardly continue to exist. A person must be acquisitive at least to some degree in order to sustain life with food, shelter, clothing and other necessities. When an attribute is so essential to survival of the individual or of the species, it is logical to regard that attribute as both inherently natural *and desirable*. This conclusion seems entirely appropriate with respect to acquisitivity in humans.

Yet that has not been the case in many instances. Even such a generous and careful thinker as C. S. Lewis appears to have treated acquisitivity as something akin to a necessary evil, but necessary only to a point. Again in *Mere Christianity*, Lewis writes about "The Great Sin" as follows: "Nearly all those evils in the world which people put down to greed or selfishness are really far more the result of Pride."[19] Lewis explains "the great sin" of pride further:

"Greed will certainly make a man want money, for the sake of a better house, better holidays, better things to eat and drink. But only up to a point. What is it that makes a man with 10,000 [pounds sterling] a year anxious to get 20,000 [pounds sterling] a year? It is not the greed for more pleasure. Ten thousand [pounds sterling] will give all the luxuries that any man can really enjoy. It is Pride—the wish to be richer than some other rich man, and (still more) the wish for power."[20]

This, of course, is quite a powerful indictment of acquisitivity. Even the desire of a person for a better home, more leisure and better food is attributed to the motive of sinful greed.

But what is worse, any desire to acquire beyond the extent of luxurious consumption is chalked up to the worst sin in the realm of Christian morality. Pride. This is no small matter. In Lewis' careful assessment, Christian teachers regard pride as the essential vice, the utmost evil, the complete anti-God state of mind, leading to all other vices. As compared to pride, "[u]nchastity, anger, greed, drunkenness, and all that, are mere fleabites."[21]

That any degree of appreciation of acquisitivity may run afoul of Christian teaching should come as no surprise. The ministry of Jesus of Nazareth 2,000 years ago left a legacy that appears to be at odds at several important junctures with the suggestion that acquisitive conduct is divinely intended and beneficial to all mankind.

Jesus is said to have taught that the rich man who would tear down his barns to build larger ones for his bountiful harvests is foolish, for he may die that night; that a man should not seek material things, but the kingdom of God; that no thought should be given to the need for food or clothing, since God provides even for the fowls of the air; and that the lilies of the field neither toil nor spin, and yet Solomon in all his glory was not arrayed so magnificently.[22] Jesus said that a rich man is due woe, because he has already received his consolation.[23] And, of course, there is the admonition that it is easier for a camel to pass through the eye of a needle than for a rich man to enter the Kingdom of Heaven.

Yet He also taught that for one who seeks the Kingdom of God, "all these things shall be added unto you."[24] And from the time of Abraham chronicled in the Old Testament, one who follows the Lord may prosper through long and diligent effort and be "blessed in all things."[25]

Nevertheless, at the very least, some considerable effort will be required to determine on what basis, if any, acquisitivity is reconcilable with Christianity.

If, indeed, greed or pride is the motivation of any and all persons who aspire to a better home, better living conditions, or even for "more" beyond the needs of personal consumption, then all entreaties on behalf of acquisitivity are unworthy and should be abandoned. But since that is not necessarily the case in every circumstance, or probably even in most instances, then each case deserves examination and consideration on its own merits.

At first blush, Jim Clark, the somewhat unlikely founder of Silicon Graphics, Netscape and Healtheon, seems to bolster C. S. Lewis' conclusions about human motives. The author Michael Lewis reports that, when Clark was discharged from the Navy and returned to Plainview, Texas, he aspired to someday earn $50,000 per year. When Clark founded Silicon Graphics, he hoped someday to have $10,000,000. When he left Silicon Graphics in search of an idea that would become Netscape, Clark wanted to be worth $100,000,000. When he set out to organize Healtheon, Clark said "I just want to have a billion dollars, after taxes. Then I will be satisfied." And when he had three billion dollars, he said he would be satisfied when he had more money than Larry Ellison, founder of Oracle Software Corporation, who had nine billion.[26]

Does this prove C. S. Lewis' point about sinful pride? Perhaps not. Author Michael Lewis observes that Jim Clark appears to voice and use many such considerations as money and resentment of others as "little tricks on himself" to provide motives for his continued productivity. Lewis reasons that Clark obviously "couldn't stop using technology to change the world, so he needed an excuse not to stop."[27] Apparently the excuse picked by Clark, at least the one announced to the world, is that he has done it for the money.

But is that not the motive that Jim Clark understands society finds most credible? If Clark stated clearly in a press release that he created three different billion dollar companies, and continues to try to do something even bigger again and again, because he wants to create substantial and lasting benefits for society, what would be the public response? Most likely that Jim Clark is a liar and a hypocrite. So Clark is, from this viewpoint, taking the easy way out and preserving his credibility by indicating that he does what he does for the money out of personal greed.

Although Clark himself may fully believe it, the "I did it for the money" statement is quite possibly a cover story, since in at least one sense it is not particularly credible. When a person has three billion dollars, is it likely that he will continue to engage perpetually in intellectual and spiritual insomnia for additional money that he could not possibly have the opportunity to spend and enjoy?

No, it is unlikely. The probable roots of his conduct relate to a keen intellect raised in such economic scarcity that even in the 1990's his mother and sister were almost literally faced with "cooking the cat" until a gift of Netscape stock lifted living standards.[28]

A person who lives his youth in such circumstances, punctuated by a drunken father followed by a fatherless home,[29] quite understandably will have an acute appreciation of the need for innovation, creativity and productivity. And that person will certainly exhibit an intense recognition that acquisitivity feeds resources to the economic process. After his childhood and youthful experiences, it would almost have been shocking and disappointing if Clark had "kicked back" and quit work to live life as a consumer after making his first $10 million or $100 million.

Regardless of the correct interpretation of Jim Clark's motives as they exist from time to time, one person's efforts and actions motivated for good purposes should not be condemned because another person's similar conduct had bad motives. C. S. Lewis himself taught that the motive for conduct is all-important in judging the morality of an act.

"[T]he truth is that right actions done for the wrong reason do not help to build the internal quality or character called a 'virtue,' and it is this quality or character that really matters."[30]

Two people may do the same act for entirely different reasons, and one rightly will be adjudged honorable while the other is reprehensible. For example, one person might kill another to prevent the murder of a woman or child, while another person might kill to take the victim's watch or wallet.

Lewis also teaches another important point by distinguishing "between differences in morality and differences in belief about facts."[31] He illustrates his lesson by discussing why witches are no longer executed in England.

"[S]urely the reason we do not execute witches is that we do not believe there are such things. If we did—if we really thought that there were people going about who had sold themselves to the devil and received supernatural powers from him in return and were using these powers to kill their neighbours or drive them mad or bring bad weather, surely we would all agree that if anyone deserved the death penalty, then these filthy quislings did. There is no difference of moral principle here: the difference is simply about a matter of fact. It may be a great advance in knowledge not to believe in witches: there is no moral advance in not executing them when you do not think they are there."[32]

This lesson has a great deal of bearing on acquisitivity and why we must endeavor to understand the facts of it better.

In a certain sense, the toiling businessmen and entrepreneurs of the late Twentieth Century are pilloried as latter day "witches," despised for their amassing of riches beyond their real needs, for their miserly shepherding of their resources, and for their endless accrual of ever more wealth. "The rich get richer, while the poor get poorer" is the battle cry of those who would do all within their power to assure that no one is very much richer than anyone else.

Despised, that is, unless and until they begin giving away substantial portions of their assets to "charitable" causes. At that moment, the greedy, miserly, selfish and prideful "witch" of a money-monger becomes better understood as actually a humanitarian, a philanthropic lover of his fellow man. The re-enactment of this scenario in countless cases ought to teach as much about society and its mistaken and unwise treatment of those who acquire wealth as it does about the wealthy.

Morality has rules of conduct not only for the wealthy, but also for those with fewer material resources. Rules about the harmful effects on human character of envy, covetousness, jealousy and pride apply to the rich, but likewise to the less rich and the poor. Those who use legislation on behalf of popular majorities to induce transfer of wealth from productive individuals to "charitable" organizations defined to the liking of the elected representatives may need to examine their own motives as they express their appreciation for the assets received.

On the other hand, a person capable of giving hard-earned assets to a charity quite likely had a motive higher and better than greed, selfishness or pride during and throughout the years of effort expended in acquiring that wealth. Surely this is at least possible. And based upon many examples of anecdotal evidence, a much higher motive for work and resource acquisition exists in case after case, regardless of whether the person winds up giving any portion of the acquired resources to charity.

Consider the life experiences and conduct of Bob and Ellen Thompson as remarkable and yet not entirely atypical examples.[33]Bob Thompson married Ellen and began a business with $3,500 in the basement of his three bedroom frame house in Belleville, Michigan, while his schoolteacher wife supported the family. The business was asphalt paving. Bob worked for 40 years making that business successful, expanding into road building. Bob and his Ellen continued to work and live in the same house, with Ellen mopping floors and washing windows even after Bob had sold the company in July, 1999.

The sale price of Bob's company was $422,000,000. When the sale was completed, Bob sent each of the company's employees a letter assuring job security and announcing that $128,000,000 of the sale price would be divided among the 550 employees of the company. More than 80 of those employees would become millionaires through Bob's allocation of the sale proceeds.

Bob explains his action, in which Ellen concurred, as follows: "People work exceedingly hard for us. It's a tough business and this is a demanding company." Bob details his meaning by describing 14 hour days, six day weeks, 99 degree weather and 300 degree asphalt. Bob notes that some individuals make a lot of money in the stock market, but emphasizes that his company was "dependent on people, *so it would just not be fair not to do it.*"

Bob and Ellen also plan to give away much of what's left of the $422 million and Bob minimizes the significance of the $128 million distributed to his employees. "I'm not trying to be a big shooter," Bob says. "A lot of people don't get the opportunity [to give a lot of money], but would if they could. This [allocating the money to his employees] didn't change my life a whole lot when you get right down to it."

Much can be learned from Bob Thompson's actions and words. Bob and Ellen worked long and hard, lived frugally, and when the big payoff came, both were concerned with *fairness*. Fairness was obviously a central concern for Bob at the time he was selling his company and collecting the sale price. Therefore, it seems reasonable to conclude that fairness was probably an important concern to him in his business dealings with others, including his employees, over the 40 years of his career. And, if a person is centrally concerned with fairness in his conduct, is it fair to him to presume that his conduct in acquiring great personal wealth by building a company worth $422 million was motivated solely, or even in substantial part, by greed? Surely not.

Bob Thompson's statement that his distribution of $128 million to his employees "didn't change my life a whole lot" says a whole lot about Bob's attention to moral considerations in his personal conduct. Bob is saying that he recognizes that his gift, though large in absolute terms of dollars, was not so large as to cause him or his wife or children personal hardship. Therefore, Bob is acknowledging that, from a moral viewpoint, a poor man who makes a relatively meager gift, but at greater personal sacrifice to himself, is perhaps performing a more charitable and selfless act. Bob Thompson is clearly a person who has a careful eye, not only for the line of an asphalt paved road or the bottom line of a financial statement, but also for the finer points of moral conduct among human beings.

Review the candid remarks of individuals who continue working long hours for years after meeting all of their own needs for wealth and you will find a notable pattern. Almost to a person, although not necessarily in the same words, each will state that he or she does not work for the money; the money simply happens or comes because of what the person does; work continues because the work provides a feeling of usefulness, and is what they want to do in their life; the joy has been in the journey, not in the wealth attained at the end of the trip.

Yet the elite of society, at least those whose world view is from the left wing of the political spectrum, continue to treat the wealthy as forgiven and redeemed only to the extent of their gifts to charitable or other socially acceptable causes.

A typical though extreme example (in terms of the vast amount of resources involved) of this common phenomenon is the case of Bill Gates, the relatively youngish founder of the computer software company known as Microsoft. Due to his success as the Chief Executive Officer and principal stockholder of Microsoft, Bill became by reputation the wealthiest man in the world.

In 1999, Bill's representatives announced that he would donate $100,000,000,000 of his assets to a family foundation organized for the purpose of supporting improvements in access to education by members of minority and ethnic groups. Bill reportedly will rely upon his father to arrange the affairs of the charitable foundation.

In announcing the remarkably large prospective donation, the senior Mr. Gates said of his son's generosity words to the effect that: "perhaps this will persuade those who have accused my son of having no compassion for the less fortunate to reconsider." Since this particular gift was itself an addition to a total of $17,000,000,000 previously committed to endow the Gates Family Foundation, the senior Gates may have foreseen that his statement reflected wishful thinking.

These occurrences raise several points that deserve identification and examination. First, clearly the weight of public opinion as expressed through the elite media or otherwise has a powerful impact upon individuals such as Bill Gates who are successful in acquiring resources. In this particular case at least, public opinion, if not pressure, played a significant role in persuading a very wealthy man to give a very large portion of his wealth to charity.

If Mr. Gates felt pressure of that nature, we may reasonably expect that many others with less wealth would feel similar pressure. The manner in which that pressure is brought to bear may involve communication of how good and deserving the charities are, but also how bad and selfish are the private uses of the resources owned. This is, if anything, an understatement of the treatment of the wealthy by society. After all, the pressures to give away $100,000,000,000 must be quite acute if a person is to be moved from thought to action.

Secondly, one of the primary ways pressure is brought to bear in such cases is through the government power of tax legislation. Tax laws of the United States, for example, take more than half of the value of accumulated assets upon death of the owner, subject to significant offsets when the owner has donated assets to charity.

Of course, the tax laws further define the nature of charities that qualify for such donations, thereby completing another link in the chain by which government determines how assets should be removed from one ownership and transferred to another favored by the government. This feature of the tax laws has the unfortunate side effect of clouding the understanding of motives of the donor in making the contribution to charity.

Those who believe the acquisition of wealth is motivated by greed or worse may contend that the charitable donor remains as greedy as ever, but the tax laws were successful in causing the greedy rich person to disgorge some of his assets for the greater charitable good. Or the argument is advanced that the assets donated to charity would otherwise have been due the government in estate or death taxes, so it is really the government's money going to the charity; therefore, the government rightly ought to specify which charity is acceptable.

It seems to be true enough that Mr. Gates, or anyone else with accumulated wealth, would have to pay substantially more in death taxes to the government if the charitable donation is not made in advance of death. That is clearly the plan and strategy of government legislators who have enacted the tax laws, purportedly to reflect the views of the public majority. By creating a charitable foundation or otherwise making a charitable donation, the donor achieves some greater degree of continued control over the future use of the donated assets than would be the case if the same assets were simply paid to the government as death taxes.

Since these tax laws are the reality, we must presume that such considerations played at least some role in the creation of such a substantial foundation as the one announced on behalf of Microsoft's Mr. Gates. To the extent that tax consequences may be viewed as involving motives of acquisitivity, greed, selfishness or pride, the purely charitable intent of such donations of resources is qualified.

But to what effect? Is a charitable intent the highest and best moral conduct in all circumstances? Again, C. S. Lewis writes that charity in the sense of giving to the poor "is an essential part of Christian morality."[34] At the same time, Lewis would not advise that a man should act imprudently or intemperately by giving so much to charity that his own family would starve. Particularly this is so if the motive for his excessive generosity was to gain the love and adoration of the public for being such a charitable person.

Since the welfare of a person's own dependents belongs somewhere upon or above the plane of charity as a proper cause for the use of a person's resources, is there any other equally or more compelling use? In the context of this discussion of acquisitivity in human nature, the first use that ought to be examined is the one determined by the manner in which the resources were acquired.

The design of human nature seems to intend for more resources to be drawn to the person who can be most productive and creative with them. Those productive and creative uses, therefore, may be the highest and best purposes to be achieved with those resources.

The question must be raised whether the interests of mankind would be better served if the resources acquired by Bill Gates, for example, are used by him for his productive and creative purposes rather than being redistributed into charitable organizations for other uses. The case to be made that society would benefit more by Bill Gates keeping his money and using it productively rather than donating it to charity runs much along the lines of arguments made by the antagonist Undershaft in Shaw's play *Major Barbara.*

The keenness of the debate between daughter Barbara and father Undershaft is remarkable. Undershaft chides Barbara for her devotion to saving the souls of the poor through use of bread, treacle and religion, while he can do much better in achieving their redemption by giving them jobs in his armaments factories.

Undershaft argues that poverty is the worst of crimes; that all other crimes are virtues beside it. The poor are a far worse blight upon society than crime, he asserts. There are millions of poor, abject, dirty, ill-fed, ill-clothed people, Undershaft says, who "kill the happiness of society: they force us to do away with our own liberties and to organize unnatural cruelties for fear they should rise against us and drag us down into their abyss."

Undershaft himself was a dangerous man, he asserts, while he remained poor, but after acquiring wealth he became a useful, beneficent, kindly person, which is the history of most self-made millionaires. Undershaft claims that he saves the souls of Barbara and the poor from the seven deadly sins of food, clothing, firing, rent, taxes, respectability and children. "Nothing can lift those seven millstones from the neck of man but money; and the spirit cannot soar until they are lifted."[35]

The arguments made by Undershaft are partly obfuscated by the context of the character who presents them, since his livelihood and many of the premises he asserts are so repugnant to ordinary people. Undershaft is completely unapologetic about his creation of weapons of war and mass destruction. He calls himself a "profiteer in mutilation and murder," remarking that "I find myself in a specially amiable humor just now because, this morning, down at the foundry, we blew twenty-seven dummy soldiers into fragments with a gun which formerly destroyed only thirteen."[36]

Such apparent callousness towards others is juxtaposed with arguments that the guns he produces empower otherwise helpless men to pull down tyrannical regimes and claim the rights of freedom, while a democratic vote can only change the names of cabinet members.[37] Throughout the entire presentation of arguments by Undershaft and the opposing protagonists of morality and righteousness, both he and they openly concede and assert that Undershaft is a thoroughly wicked person.

Accepting drink from a vessel as corrupted as that depicted through Undershaft cannot be less than repulsive. Yet the seemingly universal abhorrence of poverty compels attention to the arguments he presents.

Bill Gates, by comparison, would have considerably lighter baggage to carry in attempting to redeem the value of his life's work. Gates has provided jobs directly to tens of thousands and indirectly to countless others. The jobs created enable many of the employed individuals to support themselves and their families by the power of their intellects rather than the strength of their backs.

The technology created through Microsoft to improve the operational capabilities of computers, particularly those small enough for individual use known as personal computers, has increased the productivity of millions of individuals. That productivity, in turn, helped to fuel a revolution in computer technology and in communications. The resulting sharp decreases in the costs of computing power and communications are already providing the prospects of unimaginable informational resources available to millions of people throughout the world. This information itself will renew the productivity cycle by enabling each person to better use his own abilities to improve his circumstances.

Bill Gates' contribution to these progressive events occurred within a time span of about 20 years. During that period, the acquisitive process of the market has moved additional resources to him in unprecedented quantities. The acquired resources exceed even the astounding amounts produced in previous generations through the mining of natural resources and the construction of transportation infrastructure.

The premise has been asserted that the natural characteristic of human acquisitivity is designed to bring those additional resources to the person who can be the most creative and productive in their use. Whether Mr. Gates' most productive years are behind or ahead of him is undeterminable at this time. If, indeed, his most productive years have already occurred, the natural process of acquisitivity would begin to disburse portions of his assets elsewhere. On the other hand, few would dispute that the enormous additional assets now at his disposal would put him in a better position at this time to influence future innovations than when he began with essentially no assets as a Harvard University freshman student dropout.

As with Undershaft's weapons of war, the technology contributed by Bill Gates may be used for good or for evil purposes. Operating systems for computers may be used to launch nuclear missiles for the defense or for the destruction of freedom and democracy.

But that is true of every creative innovation, so long as human beings retain independence of thought and action to choose whether to do right or wrong. The music of Beethoven may be enjoyed by a tyrannical dictator and by masses of hardworking people who strive for increased civility and inspiration in their lives.

The creative innovator cannot be asked to withhold his work because another person may misuse it. To the contrary, if the survival of mankind is truly in the balance, as indeed it must be in the longer term, then society ought to hope for and encourage the innovation. The greater the pace of innovation, the greater the hope for humanity.

If that argument is valid, then society should hope that Bill Gates would keep his money and continue to do his best to use it as productively as possible. Instead, Gates' announcement of his intended charitable activities had hardly been expressed before he was subjected to public demonstrations by prospective beneficiaries protesting that his proposed gifts should be made more immediately, and with different criteria for beneficiaries than he had envisioned.

Charity undoubtedly will continue to have a proper role in moral conduct. But the extent to which a person should remove assets from productive purposes and expend them for other uses, whether for consumption or for charity, is a question of considerable importance to society. A related question of equal significance is whether government should be encouraging or requiring the removal of assets from productive uses through the tax laws.

Assume that all accumulated resources were to be distributed equally to every living person. That would seem the most charitable thing that could be done, but would society be better off for it? The great majority of people around the world would have more money for consumption for a short while, and much suffering would be alleviated.

But unless human nature were completely reconstructed, or governmental restrictions were totally effective, acquisitivity would again begin the process of directing those resources to the persons who could use them most productively. While that is occurring, however, human progress would be delayed immensely in every field as our most talented individuals struggled to obtain resources necessary to survive, much less bring to fruition their innovative ideas.

That is only the short-term downside of such wholesale charity by society. The long-term implication of such a drastic setback in the prospects for progress in innovation is, of course, that it might make the crucial difference in whether humans survive on the planet.

If wholesale charity by the entire society is a bad idea, as it appears to be, then society ought to rethink its public policies that attempt to extract charity from individuals in specific cases. The particular cases in which government is most forceful, and most successful, are those cases in which the donors are the most wealthy, that is, the donors have been the most successful persons in acquiring resources.

A primary argument against wholesale charity by society is based upon the counter-productive effects on progress caused by depriving innovative persons of resources needed to implement their ideas. A further argument against the wholesale charity described is that it would require government confiscation of private property; otherwise, it would never occur. Such government power exceeds what is expressly permitted by the U.S. Constitution and is so Orwellian as to surpass the authority any government should hold.

To the extent these arguments are valid, the present public policies of the United States that extract charitable contributions at the point of confiscatory income taxes or death taxes appear to strike very close to the heart of society's best hopes for human progress and survival.

This is not to argue against charity. As C. S. Lewis wrote, charity is and will remain an essential part of Christian morality. This is so for two reasons: first, for the betterment of the character and redemption of the soul of the donor, and secondly for the aid of those in need.

Tax induced charity does nothing for the character or soul of the legislator, who gives nothing of his own in enacting the law. The enacted law colors or controls the motives of the donor, thereby depriving at least in part the character building and redeeming qualities of the giving experience. And, to the extent the tax law insulates the donor from communicating the generosity and spirit of Christian charity directly, the beneficiary is deprived of the cleansing and uplifting understanding that assistance has come from a generous and willing heart and hand.

Like every other person, Bill Gates is subject to the natural laws of human conduct. He should not lie, cheat or steal. He should not kill another person except in defense of his own or another's life, or in the service of his country. He should not be selfish, greedy or prideful. He should use his best abilities to determine right from wrong, and then he should have the fortitude to do what is right. He should strive to maintain humility in all things. He should be charitable. As should we all.

But in struggling to measure up to these considerable requirements, Mr. Gates need not concede that his conduct in being acquisitive has been wrong. To the contrary, he may rightly take solace in understanding that a natural design, perhaps even a divine design, has placed the extraordinary resources that have come to him in his hands to be put to their most productive uses.

This does not mean that productivity or acquisitivity can rightly be put above all else in life, any more than love or charity or any other one good thing can be. Christian morality does not seek the kind of person who does a certain thing because a rule says he must, but rather the sort of person who puts all the rules together in his understanding and, as a consequence, thinks and wants to do the thing that ought to be done in every instance. Acquisitivity has a rightful place in that type of thinking and conduct.

The failure of public discourse to acknowledge and understand acquisitivity in human nature and its beneficial role for society is the source of at least occasional personal confusion and disarray. This is probably true at all economic levels to a greater extent than can be readily demonstrated, but has greater visibility and garners more attention when high income individuals are involved.

In the year 2000, the geographic area centered in San Jose, California, known as Silicon Valley has experienced exceedingly rapid economic growth in its industries producing high technology products. The resulting environment includes ultra high real estate prices, a shortage of affordable housing, and new millionaires produced at a rate estimated at 64 per day.

Clinical psychologists practicing in the region call attention to a malady suffered by some newly wealthy individuals called Sudden Wealth Syndrome. SWS is characterized by symptoms including anxiety and depression suffered after abrupt changes in life circumstances due to acquisition of great wealth, often at a young age. Behavior patterns commonly involve a conclusion that work is no longer required, juxtaposed against worry about loss of the accumulated wealth. Binges of lavish spending for consumption are followed by substantial gifts to charity, sometimes upon advice of the clinical practitioners. Yet happiness remains illusive, and feelings of guilt about the wealth are chronic.

SWS seems to be the predictable byproduct of public discourse on the free market economic system. The intellectual left, meaning much of academia and the major media, insists that greed is the prime motivator of individuals participating in the market system. Thus, in the left's system of values, a person who gains wealth through the free market must have become wealthy through greed. In fact, the wealth itself proves the greed of the person who attains it. Feelings of guilt in a person, especially one young in age, who acquires wealth while accepting such a system of values should not be surprising.

Maintaining that system of values, the left would advise such a person that guilt feelings are entirely appropriate, and that the person certainly should be ashamed for acquiring wealth. Moreover, the afflicted person will be advised that spending lavishly will help to assuage the guilt, and giving generously to charity will help even more. Perhaps that is good advice, but perhaps not.

Each person might be better advised to understand the highly beneficial role of acquisitivity in human nature. Acquisitivity attracts resources in exchange for productive work. Productive work includes not only years of back-breaking toil, but also innovative and creative thinking combined with effective action. The market fairly determines the value of that productive work. Therefore, when resources flow to an individual through market processes, that person should have no doubts about the fairness of the value received, so long as ethical and moral standards of conduct have been observed in business relations.

Likewise, the person already successful in acquiring significant wealth need not feel guilty in making decisions whether to use it for further production, for consumption, or for gifts to charitable causes. Ethical and moral principles ought to receive due consideration, according to the beliefs of the individual. But economic principles will remain the same. If the person chooses to use the acquired resources for additional productivity, the invested resources will likely be returned and multiplied further. If the person elects consumption, the resources will flow to other more productive hands and minds. If charity is preferred, the resources again will seek more productive environs in due course.

With clearer understanding of acquisitivity, such decisions can be made without guilt necessarily being associated in the process. Whether the individual dwells in the lower, middle or upper strata of income levels, each person deserves to work, achieve and progress through productive efforts, free of indoctrination that greed and guilt must be the motive and reward of such efforts. In a society that understands and appreciates acquisitivity in human nature, Sudden Wealth Syndrome may be remedied before it occurs.

C. S. Lewis' point that we no longer execute witches because we no longer believe that such a thing as a witch exists deserves reiteration. We have not advanced morally by ceasing execution of witches as soon as we know that no such thing as a witch exists. Society has simply conformed existing moral standards to an advance in understanding of factual reality. Clearly, Lewis would contend that execution of a so-called witch when there is no genuine belief that the "witch" in fact exists is far more reprehensible morally than were the past executions that were based on belief that the condemned were actually witches.

So, if society now understands that individuals act acquisitively not out of greed but pursuant to a natural mechanism that benefits humanity, is it not morally reprehensible to continue persecuting those individuals as if they are greed-driven money-mongers? Lewis would advise that, if society understands businessmen are not really witches, and never were, then society must stop condemning businessmen as witches or society will be lost morally.

Society, particularly the intellectual and government elite, must begin to acknowledge that individuals have been practicing acquisitivity, not greed (or witchcraft), and that the natural human characteristic of acquisitivity is a fundamentally significant benefactor of society. With those acknowledgements, the persecution of individual business acumen through public policy will cease.

Six

Public Policy Reform

Gould, Oklahoma, in the south central United States, is a town of decaying storefronts, surrounded by parched brown fields during late August. Over the weekend of such a time in 1999, the local banker Rick Holder was out on his cattle ranch when he received a call from a local friend. The friend had news: he was suddenly rich. In fact, he and 11 other local residents were suddenly rich.

The 12 friends had bought the winning ticket in the $23,000,000 Texas Lottery jackpot announced the previous night. The caller wanted to place the ticket in a safe deposit box at Holder's bank for safekeeping. The news report of the event stated: "The reality of winning a fortune is slowly sinking in for the 12 men and women in this 250-resident town." And so, too, does the reality begin to sink in for the remaining 238 residents of Gould, of Oklahoma, and of America.

The "reality" created by the Texas Lottery, the California "Lotto" and every other State-run or government authorized gambling enterprise encourages each citizen to take his hard earned wages and spend it, not on food, clothing, shelter or education, but on gambling for the chance to become extremely wealthy. The funds to make the "winner" wealthy can come from only one source, of course. That source is the pocket of each "loser" who will be even poorer for participation in the government-sponsored scheme. In the process, let there be no doubt, the governments involved and their favored intermediaries will extract substantial portions of the gambling proceeds as their own rewards for facilitating the activity.

What lesson should the residents of Gould learn from this government conduct? Certainly the heavy advertising used by every state-run gambling operation leaves no doubt about the message it hopes to convey: No one gets rich by working; your one chance to be rich is by luck; every dollar you can spare should be spent on the chance that you will be the lucky winner! Is that responsible, or even defensible, public policy?

The customary answer of government, although sometimes couched in different terms, is that good can be accomplished by the expenditure of public funds, so the method of raising the funds is beside the point. The argument is even advanced as to gambling, or "gaming" as its proponents deceptively call it, that public funds raised through gambling are actually more benign than taxes because the funds are contributed "voluntarily" rather than by mandate.

While it is true that taxes bear the stamp of police power enforcement and gambling does not, at least it can be argued with some degree of substance that taxes are the price we pay for civilization. The encouragement of gambling, on the contrary, appears to be entirely inimical to the interests of society.

Taxes, and particularly so-called "progressively" higher marginal tax rates on higher income citizens, create a disincentive against working to generate more income. However, the encouragement of gambling strikes directly at the core of the work ethic, without which a society cannot advance or even survive. Yet all levels of American government are plunging headlong into precisely that approach to public policy.

You might expect that the cultural institutions of American society that have provided the foundations of past successes would raise formidable obstacles to the adoption of such public policies. The literature of the Catholic Church, for example, has been especially expressive in deploring the perceived disparities in income and wealth among individuals produced by the capitalist or free enterprise system of commerce. Logically, one would suppose then that Catholicism would stand as a bulwark against state-sponsored gambling, since the very object of such a scheme is to collect money from many individuals in order to make one person very wealthy by chance.

But the sad fact is that the Catholic Church has hardly been heard at all, and mainstream Protestantism has likewise been largely silent, on the issue of the spread of state-authorized gambling. The gambling phenomenon cannot have gone entirely unnoticed, so the silence of the mainstream churches amounts to tacit approval in the eyes of many people. In the absence of an express view, one may speculate that the church hierarchies, like so many of their counterparts in the business community, prefer to be on friendly terms with their governmental regulators. Accordingly, government influence may have again succeeded in co-opting a potentially important voice of a private institution.

Only the more fundamentalist evangelical branches of the Christian churches have been heard to any important effect. Unfortunately, as is often the case on any subject of public importance, the viewpoints of the fundamentalist churches are frequently marginalized by the mainstream media as "Bible Belt" extremism.

Yet the threat to the success of America as a productive society posed by widespread gambling is quite real on a completely non-sectarian level. If the spread of gambling as a family based activity is as successful as the gambling "industry" hopes and intends to be, the decline of the work ethic and, thus, of American society, could be steep and consequential. In that event, the consequences will be felt by all, not merely by the gamblers or by the "moral majority."

The promotion of gambling as a popular activity of the people is only one of myriad ways in which governments engage in conduct arguably counter-productive to sound public policy. A means frequently used by governments to influence the conduct of people is, of course, the adoption of tax laws and regulations. These are the legislative and administrative tools by which any government tells its constituents "we will take more of your money if you act in a certain way," or "we will take less of your money if you act in a certain way."

Many of the messages presently sent by governments to the American people through the tax laws advise against productivity, earning of income and acquisition or ownership of property. In light of what we now know and are capable of knowing about the central importance of human acquisitivity to the success and survival of civilization, our public policies as expressed through the tax laws ought to be reconsidered and realigned accordingly.

The facts are that most taxes in the United States are laid upon income produced through work and labor, and are laid most heavily upon those who earn the most income. Each person who works for wages must pay specially designed employment taxes to support government sponsored retirement, health care and disability programs. Taxes are also laid against property owned by the taxpayer, both during the owner's life and upon his death. At the same time, those who earn little income or none at all are not taxed at all, or are actually paid an "earned income tax credit" and other benefits by the government. And, of course, the government gets the money to pay those benefits from other individuals who work, earn income and pay taxes.

If a person earns income, he must pay taxes on it. If he then invests the remaining funds in a productive trade or business, the trade or business must pay taxes on any income earned. And, in addition, the investor must pay taxes on any increase in the value of the invested funds as a "capital gain" as soon as the gain is realized. These governmental actions in imposing taxation are unmistakably unfriendly to productive work and investment of capital, and can be interpreted as official encouragement of idleness among the citizenry.

If such tax laws were the only means available for raising public funds, they might be pardoned as necessities. But that is most certainly not the case. Other designs for taxation readily come to mind.

However, in arriving at the best conceived designs, we should first recall that acquisitivity as a characteristic of human nature may serve the role of a natural mechanism for distribution of resources to those most able to use them in a productive manner. That natural mechanism requires individual freedom to function at its best, and is disrupted to the extent government interdicts and redirects the flow of resources to politically favored groups or uses.

Individual freedom to acquire resources carries with it the freedom to determine the use of the resources acquired, whether for production, consumption or otherwise. The arena of individual freedom within which that determination of uses of resources is made, rather than the acquisition of resources, ought to be the focus of attention in the design and collection of taxes.

So long as the acquired resources are used in productive ways, the resources should not be taken by government as taxes. So long as the resources are directed to charitable uses, no taxes should interfere or discourage the use. But if the resources are used by the acquiring individual for personal consumption, then the government could appropriately levy a tax on the amount consumed without interfering unreasonably in the natural process of resource allocation.

The idea of taxing consumption rather than production is not new. But perhaps something is added to the foundation for such an approach to tax policy by better understanding the role of acquisitivity in human nature. So long as greed is seen as, or at least is said to be, the sole motivator of productive conduct, then productivity will remain the easy target of the tax legislators. But when acquisitivity in human nature is correctly understood as truly a major benefactor of society, then perhaps there will be room for hope that meaningful tax reform is actually achievable.

Such concerns as tax reform have real consequences for the success of society as a whole and for the success of governments. These consequences extend beyond the mere penalties and benefits dealt to one class or another by opposing political factions.

Peter F. Drucker, the prolific writer and teacher called a "social analyst and management philosopher" by his colleagues and peers, recently provided a brief retracement of the decline of England as a predominant world industrial power after 1850.[38] Professor Drucker importantly noted that the major reason generally acknowledged for this decline was neither economic nor technological, but *social*.

The social reason for England's decline was that the technologist was not permitted to become a "gentleman" in English society. Despite the social elevation of the scientist, the technologist remained a tradesman, and society eventually paid the price for this lack of foresight. Drucker relates this historical experience in arriving at his central concern that, in America, "a drastic change in the social mind-set is required" to prevent the United States from becoming the England of the Twenty-first Century.

The need for "drastic change" in American thinking is based in Professor Drucker's conclusions that the Information Revolution is actually a Knowledge Revolution, the key to which is cognitive science, not electronics. Drucker contends that when the initial economic and financial boom of the Knowledge Revolution is dissipated, and corporate stock options are no longer so lucrative, the arduous work of knowledge professionals will not be so attractive. Thereafter, maintaining American leadership in this revolution will ultimately depend upon the manner in which society deals with knowledge professionals—whether they continue to be treated as "employees" or are elevated to some higher status. Drucker concludes as follows:

"Increasingly, performance in these new knowledge-based industries will come to depend on running the institution so as to attract, hold, and motivate knowledge workers. When this can no longer be done *by satisfying knowledge workers' greed, as we are now trying to do,* it will have to be done by satisfying their values, and by giving them social recognition and social power."[39]

Again, even such an insightful and experienced "social analyst and management philosopher" as Professor Drucker appears to attribute entirely to personal greed a knowledge worker's desire to acquire property.

Sadly, this is precisely the existing social mind-set that is in greatest need of drastic change. Drastic change in the social mind-set will not be achieved by merely calling the knowledge worker an executive or a partner rather than an employee, but continuing to regard him as a greedy money-monger. As Drucker himself says, there must be social acceptance of the knowledge professionals and their values.

What are those values? Anecdotal evidence is endless because each person acts upon many motivations that may vary from minute to minute. Particular experiences, however, offer a potential to reveal wider patterns of behavior. One briefly described example is compelling in its illustration of the influence of values in the personal and professional conduct of knowledge workers.

During the 1970's, Herbert Sullivan worked at Columbia University performing studies centered upon parallel processors in computers. In 1979, Sullivan founded a small private corporation to advance his work. At about the same time, Sullivan began a professional collaboration and personal friendship with Peter C. Patton. Patton likewise had earned the award of a doctorate in computer science and shared Sullivan's interest in improving the performance of computers.

By the mid-1980's, Dr. Sullivan had raised sufficient capital to begin construction of a super-computer. However, the super-computer project was never successfully completed. The project's failure was due primarily to a collapse of the corporation's share price as a result of false and fraudulent statements critical of the corporation's technology publicized by a stock manipulator unrelated to Sullivan or the corporation.[40] As of 1995, Dr. Sullivan's corporation still had no commercially viable product. During those difficult years, Dr. Patton collaborated with his friend on a *pro bono* basis.

In 1995, Dr. Sullivan's corporation was awarded its first patent based on innovations in methods for instructing computers to perform their assigned tasks. In 1996, in recognition of his contributions and as incentive for further efforts, Dr. Patton was awarded warrants to purchase 200,000 shares of stock in Dr. Sullivan's corporation for a strike price of 25 cents per share, which was just under the market price of the stock at the time.

In 1999, subsequent to the passing of Dr. Sullivan during the previous year, the corporation was renamed ANTS Software.com, Inc. ANTS was chosen as an acronym for the innovative Asynchronous Non-preemptive Tasks method of programming computers derived from Dr. Sullivan's theories and work.

On January 31, 2000, ANTS Software.com announced that its management and board of advisors (including Dr. Patton) on that date had witnessed a demonstration of the ANTS software technology in which one million transactions had been processed in less than one second. As of that date, the official world record for computer speed in processing transactions as recorded with the Transaction Processing Performance Council (TPC) was 135,815 transactions per minute, or 2,263 transactions per second. The official record was shared by IBM and Groupe Bull, which had reported their achievements to TPC on October 29 and November 5, 1999, respectively.

On February 2, 2000, ANTS Software announced Dr. Patton's resignation from its board of advisors. After an adverse reaction in the market price of ANTS common shares, ANTS Software issued a further explanation of Dr. Patton's departure on February 7.

Dr. Patton had resigned because his primary employment was as Chief Technologist and Senior Vice President for International Business Development of Lawson Software. Lawson Software's financial software program had been used in the demonstration of ANTS technology. Due to the possibility of future business dealings between ANTS Software and Lawson Software, Dr. Patton had chosen to resign from his advisory post at ANTS Software in order to avoid the potential conflict of interests in his future work. In submitting his resignation from the board of advisors of ANTS Software, Dr. Patton also waived his rights under the warrants to purchase 200,000 shares of ANTS for 25 cents per share.

By February 2, 2000, the date of Dr. Patton's resignation, the market price of shares of ANTS Software had risen above $50.00 and was about $40.00 per share on the date of his waiver. By his waiver, Dr. Patton effectively gave back to the corporation securities valued by the market at about $8,000,000 on that date, and potentially worth much, much more. Upon informal inquiry regarding his motives, Dr. Patton explained that, at his age, money did not mean a lot and he believed his integrity and impartiality were more important considerations.

Integrity and impartiality are values that the Christian author C. S. Lewis would include within the concept of the Cardinal Virtue of Justice (the remaining three Cardinal Virtues being Prudence, Temperance and Fortitude).[41] The virtue of Justice means a sense of fairness and, according to Lewis, "includes honesty, give and take, truthfulness, keeping promises, and all that side of life."[42]

Lewis describes the Cardinal Virtues as recognized by all civilized people. Based on what we know of his conduct, Dr. Patton clearly is one of those people, at least insofar as his sense of Justice is concerned. And with his sense of Justice so finely tuned, the likelihood that he holds similarly high regard for Prudence, Temperance and Fortitude seems a very strong probability.

Indeed, Dr. Patton's conduct may be extraordinary as well as exemplary. But his conduct is more logically representative of the values shared by his colleagues and peers. A sense of acquisitivity undoubt-edly is within that penumbra of values. This is reflected by the issuance of the warrants and remains so nonetheless despite Dr. Patton's later waiver. Dr. Patton's relinquishment of the valuable war-rants seems to demonstrate his conclusion that the resources could be used more productively in the future endeavors of ANTS Software than by him personally.

If the values reflected in the conduct of Herbert Sullivan and Peter C. Patton are indicative of the values of the knowledge community in gen-eral, the society at large should hold no hostility towards them. Indeed, society at large might well benefit by embracing them.

Sinful greed may make an appearance within the knowledge community on any occasion, as with all humankind. But greed is not fundamentally at the core of intellectual innovation, any more than it is at the core of manual labor. Acquisitivity, by contrast, is at the core of both intellectual innovation and manual labor.

Social acceptance of values will come on a genuine basis only through better understanding of the principles of conduct which underlie them. Those values almost assuredly include, as well they ought, the principles that work and productivity are good in and of themselves; that productive individuals are benefactors of society as a whole; that accumulation of resources is inherently necessary for improved productivity; and that a person rightly deserves to be materially rewarded in fair proportion to contribution. Whether that material reward is then used in further production or diverted to personal consumption is a private exercise of personal freedom by the individual concerning his own property.

Something more must be said about acquisitivity in relation to the values of knowledge workers and all others who create, innovate and produce. Acquisitivity in human nature combines with the human sense of justice to produce a deep conviction that compensation received must be within fair proportion to be contribution made, or at

least in fair proportion to the compensation gained by others participating in the same endeavor. The fact that others had achieved greater
financial gain from Silicon Graphics, Inc., than founder Jim Clark
offended deeply his sense of justice. In founding Netscape, therefore,
Clark insisted upon terms that better served his acquisitive interests.

If no one had made money in the creation of Silicon Graphics, Clark
may still have had a burning desire to create another "new, new thing,"
but his sense of justice would not have been offended. The sense of
justice, or fairness, will be a fundamental element of the values of
knowledge workers that will make new titles inadequate to satisfy their
demands for proper treatment. Human acquisitivity and sense of
justice will require that each person receive compensation in
proportion to the financial gains realized from the contribution made,
or the system will offend and dissatisfy those most critical to the
system's long term success.

The potential for improved appreciation of knowledge professionals
is what a proper understanding of acquisitivity in human nature brings
to the table. And, of course, the set of principles stated above may right-
fully be claimed not only by knowledge professionals, but also by workers, innovators and producers of every stripe.

When American society espouses these values through its mainstream media and through its enacted public policies, then all those
who contribute to the success of society will be elevated to their proper
levels of recognition. If that can be achieved, America will continue its
leadership in world technological innovation.

In that enlightened circumstance, this will evolve not merely because
the United States provides a somewhat better environment for work
and productivity than other governments of the world currently allow.
American society will have made a quantum leap in advancing the
understanding of conditions that best accommodate the needs of
human nature for success and survival.

As Americans strive and reach for this new level of understanding, any degree of improved enlightenment ought to be reflected in reforms of existing public policy. No better opportunity exists than in the field of tax law.

The influence of taxes upon the lives of Americans is a matter of great consequence. The objective of tax legislators has been likened to the plucking of geese, which seeks the maximum amount of feathers with the minimum amount of hissing and pecking. Doubtless the American government abhors hissing and pecking from its citizens, but nevertheless tax legislation and regulation is used extensively in the United States to punish, control and guide individual conduct.

The Tax Foundation, a private research organization, reports that government at all levels in the United States will collect taxes equal to $10,298 per man, woman and child during the year 1999. Not every American will pay that amount, of course. Many will pay nothing, some will pay considerably more, and a few will pay much more.

In 1996, the most recent year for which the IRS has made data available, the top 50% of income earners (those with incomes over $74,481) paid 95.7% of the federal individual income tax burden, while the bottom 50% of income earners paid only 4.3% of the total income taxes collected. In 1996, the top 1% of earners (those who earned adjusted gross income over $229,230) paid 32.3% of total individual income taxes, and the top 5% of earners (5.9 million individuals who had adjusted gross incomes of $101,202 or more) paid 50.8% of total individual income taxes.

This "progressivity" in placing higher tax burdens on the highest earning individuals has increased sharply since 1980, when the top 5% of earners paid "only" 36.8% of total federal individual income taxes. Individuals in the top 1% of tax filers earned 16.0% of total adjusted gross income in 1996, but they paid 32.3% of federal individual income taxes during that year. The average effective federal individual income tax rate for this group was 29.0%. Similarly, tax filers in the top 5% of income earners earned 30.4% of total adjusted gross income during 1996, but paid 50.8% of total federal income tax collections. The average effective tax rate for this group was 24.1%.

But on the average, meaning if the total individual income taxes paid were to be divided equally by the number of potential taxpayers, taxes would consume more resources than the average person pays for food ($2,693), clothing ($1,404), and shelter ($5,833) combined. Again on the average, Americans would spend more on federal taxes alone ($7,026) than on any other major household budget item, compared to $5,833 per person for housing and household operations, $3,829 for health and medical care, $2,693 for food, $2,568 for transportation, $1,922 for recreation and $1,404 for clothing.

Of course, as discussed above, many individuals pay less in federal taxes than the above amount would suggest, and some taxpayers pay far more, due to the uneven manner in which taxes are levied and collected on the highest earners. But the amounts collected as federal taxes increased by 45% in the years between 1981 and 1999. Total taxes collected by all levels of American government have more than doubled since 1967.

These few numbers do not adequately describe the full extent of the influence tax laws have on American lives. The federal Internal Revenue Code comprises more than 2,000 pages of law, more than 6,000 pages of regulations and many volumes of rulings and cases disposing of tax issues. Americans spend an estimated 5.1 billion hours filling out income tax forms in order to comply with the law. The annual cost of these compliance efforts is estimated to be at least $135 billion and perhaps $300 billion, which is in addition to the $600 billion paid in federal income taxes.

Complexity in the tax laws regularly causes very substantial disparities in computation of tax liabilities by expert tax consultants when they are separately presented the same details of a particular taxpayer's earnings. The annual expense of operating the Internal

Revenue Service is $7.2 billion. The IRS employs more investigative agents than the Federal Bureau of Investigation and the Central Intelligence Agency combined. With 115,000 employees, the IRS is a larger employer than any but the 36 largest U.S. corporations.

The IRS has been given statutory power by Congress and the President to seize property and businesses without a prior hearing in court to collect claimed taxes. The IRS even claims the right under law to confiscate retirement assets not yet payable to a taxpayer who has not yet retired in order to satisfy a presently alleged tax liability. If the entity holding the assets claimed by the IRS, such as a pension or other retirement plan, fails to pay over the funds claimed by the IRS, that entity is itself made liable for a penalty in a sum equal to the amount owed by the allegedly delinquent taxpayer and held back from the IRS by the entity.

This is hardly the beginning of the story of the extent to which taxation affects the lives of Americans. The tax laws seek to alter individual conduct in many, many ways and do so to degrees that are not entirely decipherable. The so-called "payroll" taxes placed on those who employ others, as well as on the employed themselves, hit hard the productive activity that government professes to encourage. Government never lets the income tax or the payroll taxes get into the hands of the person who earns the money, but takes it first before the taxpayer ever sees it through "withholding" requirements placed upon the employer.

Payroll taxes are certainly not the only means by which government policy burdens employment, particularly those who employ others. For example, state governments in the early Twentieth Century adopted workers' compensation laws to limit the liability of employers for bodily injuries suffered by employees on the job. The injury might be caused by co-workers or the employees of others. Under state workers' compensation laws, the amounts of monetary benefits recoverable by an employee for serious bodily injuries are quite limited. However, more recently the federal Congress and various state legislatures have enacted other laws granting rights to employees to sue their employers without limits for infringements such as sexual harassment.

Thus, federal and state governments now typically legislate an employee right to sue without limit, even permitting punitive or exemplary damages to be awarded to punish or to make an example of an employer, for an infringement of rights in the nature of sexual discrimination or harassment. But if the same employee were to be negligently killed or seriously injured by the same person who had committed the discrimination or harassment, the employer's liability would be strictly limited by the worker's compensation laws. This is arguably an irrational public policy towards employment.

Such irrational public policies affecting employers must be rationalized by the business decisions of the affected employers. Therefore, governments should expect that an employer affected by these laws will consider the costs and benefits of hiring and retaining employees under such circumstances and will, oftentimes, conclude that employment is not wise or profitable.

That is why large employers, even in profitable times, have been seen announcing staff reductions numbering in the tens of thousands, while simultaneously showing record profits. Those employers, whether wisely or not, have likely concluded that government policies make it unwise and unprofitable to be an employer, and that they can profit more by subcontracting their work to others.

Most reprehensible in this scenario is the conduct of government officials watching the staff reduction announcements. With hand-wringing concern, they commonly express dismay that any employer would do such a thing as lay off employees during profitable times, as though government policies had nothing to do with the turn of events.

Government policies do, of course, affect the conduct of individuals, both in their personal affairs as well as in their businesses. Government legislators certainly acknowledge this reality when adopting their policies, but are much slower to do so when the policies turn out to be unwise; *i.e.*, when the resulting individual conduct is either not what the legislator envisioned or proves to be detrimental to public interests.

Acknowledgement of policy error seems to occur more promptly at the state, regional or local levels of government than at the federal level. This may be primarily because individuals and businesses can protest the locally enacted policies in various ways, including by moving to other locales. Local politicians feel the economic pain inflicted by such protests through the effects of fewer jobs and lower tax revenues. When that occurs, those political leaders (or their successors) are apt to see the light and enact measures that make their economic community more attractive to those who wish to do business.

Clearly there are numerous areas of public policy that have a great deal of room for improvement. A better understanding and apprecia-tion of acquisitivity and its role as a natural mechanism for efficient allocation of resources for production ought to be a foundation for that improvement.

No better place to begin can be found than fundamental reform of the tax laws. Presently the U.S. federal government lays the tax laws directly across the path of natural acquisitivity, collecting the highest tax rates on income earned by those taxpayers who earn the most or who own the most resources. Rather than taxing work, employment, production and earning success, the government should redirect the tax impact to fall upon consumption.

Consumption is the act of pulling resources out of the stream of pro-duction for immediate use and enjoyment. Consumption of resources to serve basic needs for survival is, of course, a central motivating force of humanity. As such, consumption in satisfying necessity is an unas-sailable (and unalienable) human right endowed in each individual by their Creator.

Yet from the current practice of public policy, taxation of necessary consumption is not off limits. Work and productivity, including the earning of wages to provide basic necessities, is presently subject to taxes, including income taxes, employment taxes and excise taxes. But taxes on consumption can be designed to allow a basic level of consumption for each individual's necessities before the tax applies, or to rebate a basic amount of consumption tax as an effective exemption of basic necessities for each individual.

That is one of the features of proposed legislation presently pending in the U.S. Congress to repeal much of the existing tax law and replace the revenue with a broad-based tax on consumption. One such bill is called the National Retail Sales Tax Act (NRST) and a second is called the Fair Tax Act.

The NRST proposes to repeal the federal income tax, the corporate tax, the capital gains tax, the estate and gift taxes, and all federal excise taxes, and to replace the revenue with a 16% tax applicable to all final sales of goods and services for consumption. The Fair Tax would repeal essentially the same existing taxes (except excise taxes) *plus* the federal payroll/employment taxes, and would replace the revenue with a 23% sales tax on consumption of goods and services.

Each of these legislative proposals intends to be "revenue neutral" in raising the same amount of federal revenue, while reforming the structure and effects of collecting the funds. Either reform likewise proposes to repeal the Sixteenth Amendment to the U.S. Constitution, which is the authority relied upon by the federal government to levy and collect income tax. After repeal of the Sixteenth Amendment, Congress could not levy the national sales tax and later reinstate the federal income tax.

The attractions of a national sales tax directed at consumption as a replacement of the present federal tax structure are numerous and appealing, and occur on several levels of concern. First and foremost is the concern for reduction in the degree of government intrusiveness in individual conduct and personal liberty. Presently the federal income tax laws require each person to detail regularly in written reports to the IRS all income received and all expenditures made to generate that income. The regulation of the manner in which such reports must be prepared and of the amount of taxes to be paid is so complex that the reporting process is very expensive and uncertain in its reliability. As a concomitant element of this revenue raising process, the IRS employs literally hundreds of thousands of agents to investigate, audit and enforce collection of allegedly due taxes.

Regardless of acclamations that the U.S. has the "largest voluntary tax compliance system in the world," the operation of the IRS has many troubling characteristics of an agency of a modern police state. The citizen must report all details of income, and failure to report will result in imprisonment by order of a federal judge according to a summary procedure known as an order to show cause re: contempt of court. A person who has filed with the IRS a written report of income has the burden of proof to establish that the report is complete and accurate. The IRS has authority by statute to seize assets and to padlock a business without seeking a court order through a hearing and due process.

All of this involves direct intrusion into individual conduct of every person and enforcement by police powers. These concerns can be eliminated almost entirely by substituting the consumption tax in place of the income tax. On its face, the proposed consumption tax reform ought to be the civil libertarian's poster child.

A consumption tax would be collected at the point of sale of the goods or services by the seller. Only the seller would be required to report and pay the collected taxes to the government. Thus, the number of returns to be filed with the government would be drastically reduced. Legislators proposing the NRST or the Fair Tax would provide for the federal government to contract with each state government to collect the federal sales tax, in exchange for payment of a small percentage of the tax collected.

The cost of tax collection by that approach would be a small fraction of the current expense of operating the IRS. The fee earned by each collecting state would significantly supplement and offset the need for other state tax revenues. Individual consumers would have to file no tax return whatsoever. The significance of the reduction in compliance costs, as well as the sheer simplicity of this tax collection system, is simply staggering in comparison to the existing federal income tax system nightmare.

This is only the beginning of the benefits of fundamental tax reform. Owing to present income tax and payroll/employment taxes directed so heavily at labor and production, manufactured goods now produced in the U.S. have cost elements that include those taxes paid for the labor of production. Federal income taxes are presently estimated to comprise about 16% of the cost of goods made in the U.S. Therefore, goods made in the U.S. have at least a 16% income tax burden when they are shipped abroad to compete in foreign markets. If those U.S.-made goods are sold here at home, they still have a 16% income tax burden that imported foreign goods do not have when competing for U.S. consumer dollars. This tax burden is a great competitive disadvantage for U.S. manufacturers, both in the U.S. market and abroad.

The public media repeatedly headline the deficit in trade balance of payments, meaning the difference in value of goods and services sold abroad as compared to the value of those imported into the U.S. Nevertheless, the same media largely fail to report or critique the negative effects of federal tax policy on the competitiveness of U.S. manufactured goods. The greater economic prosperity in the U.S., and the resulting financial capability to purchase more goods and services, explain partly the continuing experience of importing far more than we export. But the trade imbalance is undeniably made considerably worse by the tax burden imposed upon U.S.-made goods, when no such tax burden applies to foreign-made goods. Repeal of the federal income tax and/or the federal payroll taxes would alleviate this uneven tax treatment for U.S. versus foreign-made goods. A consumption tax would apply uniformly to all sales of goods sold in the U.S., whether made in the U.S. or abroad.

The impact of fundamental tax reform—meaning repeal of federal income/employment taxes and substitution of a broad-based consumption tax—has been anticipated by economists and other experienced observers. Those who have studied the subject most closely foresee a virtual renaissance in U.S. manufacturing activity as the consequence of such reform. International corporations with the business objective of making their products at the most advantageous locations in the world have expressed great affinity for establishing new plants and equipment in the U.S. if consumption based tax reform is enacted.

Such an increase in manufacturing capacity within the U.S. through deployment of new investment capital would be a godsend to the employment aspirations of many Americans. Even in a long-booming economy with reportedly low unemployment rates, young workers commonly experience considerable difficulties in gaining earning capacity sufficient to support a home and family, even after completing a college education. The remedy for such impaired earning capacity must lie very close to an increase in investment capital directed towards production requiring physical as well as intellectual output: namely, manufacturing.

Without fundamental tax reform in the nature of a consumption tax replacing the existing taxes on income and employment, a rebirth of manufacturing in the U.S. simply will not happen. The trends in the opposite direction under the present tax system are well established, and Americans cannot expect a reversal in those trends absent fundamental change.

This may explain partially the shift in public opinion against the existing tax system and in favor of fundamental tax reform in the U.S. A majority of Americans now view the existing tax system as unfair and favor fundamental reform. Indeed, a growing plurality appears to favor a broad-based consumption tax such as the Fair Tax proposal or the NRST as the preferred alternative to existing law. That view is gaining support from individuals and groups aligned with both major political parties, and appears to be favored by pivotal Republican leadership of the Ways and Means Committee in the U.S. House of Representatives as well as in the Senate. These are significant considerations and portend the existence of a real opportunity to achieve the needed reform.

A discussion of fundamental tax reform often includes reference to "flat tax" reforms of the federal income tax laws. While the flat tax proposals propose to move in the right direction by seeking greater simplicity and predictability in the effects of the tax laws, the flat tax design appears to be fundamentally flawed. First, the flat tax remains a tax on income, so the burden and intrusiveness of reporting all income remains fully in place. Second, the proposal for fewer and lower marginal tax rates might achieve a small degree of simplicity and somewhat higher productivity, but similar proposals adopted in the Tax Reform Act of 1986 were soon eroded by repeated legislative changes.

Finally, and most importantly, the significantly improved simplicity promised by flat tax proposals appears to be almost entirely illusive. The reason is that the complexity of the tax laws is caused, in major part, neither by the marginal tax rates nor by the manner in which gross income is counted and reported. The complexity arises primarily in the manner in which the expenses of producing the income are computed and deducted from the gross income. That complexity regarding treatment of business expenses is entirely necessary if the individual businesses involved are to have the flexibility required to create, to innovate and to compete in the ever-changing conditions of the free market.

If the proponents of the flat tax on income propose to simplify the tax laws by eliminating the right of individuals or businesses to deduct the expenses incurred in producing the income, then the flat tax becomes essentially a tax on gross income. For most businesses, such a tax would make their survival virtually impossible.

Consider a grocery supermarket, for example. Such markets ordinarily earn a very low margin of net profit, but seek to sell a high volume of goods in order to pay overhead expenses and increase total profits. A tax on gross income under those circumstances would punish higher volume of sales, and thereby encourage the business to shrink rather than expand. Rather than seeking to continue taxing income through such a difficult and potentially unworkable design, the flat tax proponents would seem to be better advised to join in the design of a well-considered sales tax on consumption as a full-fledged replacement of the income tax.

One further proposal for tax "reform" ought to be mentioned. A prospective candidate (since withdrawn) for the nomination of the Reform Party in the 2000 U.S. presidential election has proposed that the entire federal debt be paid by collecting a new tax. The proposed new tax would require each person or entity with a net worth of $10,000,000 or more to pay 14.2% of that net worth to the federal government. Of course, the prospective candidate hopes to entice the votes of the great majority who would not be paying the tax, and urges that paying off the federal debt in this manner would create economic expansion and boom times for all concerned.

"Soak the rich" tax proposals are almost as old as the democratic process. If the tax were collected, there is little to guarantee its use would be to pay off the existing debt. Even if that were done without the smallest Congressional divergence, consider the rejuvenated spending attitude of a Congress with no existing federal debt. Such a substantial new tax would become the recipe for even greater growth in federal spending and further growth of the role of government in society.

But the tax on wealth proposed by the Reform Party aspirant has additional fatal flaws. The Constitution does not authorize the federal government to levy such a direct tax on property or wealth. That is why the federal government could not lawfully impose a tax on income without passage of the Sixteenth Amendment. A comparable amendment to the Constitution would be required before the tax on wealth could be enforced.

Finally, the proposed tax on wealth would likely have an economic impact quite different from the boom times the political aspirant forecasts. That aspirant speaks as though the assets of the wealthy are locked away as gold coins in the vaults of misers. In reality, the resources to be collected as the new tax are presently in private ownership and invested in the economy. The proposed new tax would, if enacted and enforced, effectively suck several trillion dollars out of the private economy and put it into the hands of the federal government. The immediate and long term impacts of such government action are predictably devastating upon the private economy.

Those several trillion dollars presently at work in the private economy are creating jobs and economic growth. Those dollars are a significant portion of the resources acquired through human acquisitivity. They are the resources which feed the productive process. The political proposal that government should confiscate these resources through taxation is the essence of public policy designed to run counter to the natural mechanism for resource allocation. This is as profound an example as can be found to illustrate why better understanding of human acquisitivity is so urgently needed and potentially so beneficial to reform of public policy.

Undoubtedly, the defenders of the *status quo* are formidable, so much so that many who would favor reform shrink from the attempt. But if necessity is the mother of invention, it is likewise the platform for change of public policy. Enlightenment on the subject of acquisitivity in human nature is the tool that can enable that change to become reality.

Income and payroll taxes are certainly not the only elements of federal tax policy deserving reform. Estate (death) taxes are collected on the value of assets remaining after the death of the owner. If the value of the estate exceeds about $600,000 (which effectively exempts the great majority of individuals), the effective tax rate quickly rises to 55% of the assets.

Many family businesses, including family farms, are hit by this substantial levy of taxes at the most difficult time—upon the passing of a generation. Assets must be liquidated, or debt incurred, or both, in order to export the capital of the family to the federal government in the form of estate taxes.

This repeated destruction of the capital base of productive enterprises, large and small, cannot be reconciled with the principle that productivity and innovation should be encouraged and rewarded. Removal of more than half of the accumulated capital of any enterprise is devastating to its objectives, even if the loss of capital occurs only once in a generation.

Yet the existing policy of collecting estate taxes produces repeated examples of sale of businesses as strategic or tactical steps in "estate planning," meaning efforts to minimize or accommodate the impact of the estate tax laws. Such sales often transfer control of management to inexperienced ownership, resulting in even greater setbacks for production.

As with income taxes, estate and gift taxes ought to be repealed upon adoption of a tax designed to fall upon consumption. So long as assets are directed to use in investment or production, the government should not take any part of them, regardless of the transfer of ownership either by gift between living persons or by devise upon death. Society will be better served if those assets are kept in productive use, rather than taken by the government. However, if the benefactor by gift or through inheritance decides to turn any portion of the assets towards consumption, that portion can be appropriately subjected to the broad-based consumption tax applicable to all other similar consumption.

The tax laws are not the only aspects of public policy that impinge upon the natural mechanism for allocation of resources through individual acquisitivity and productivity. The propensity to acquire property seems to be no less persistent in governments than in individuals. Unfortunately, government has police powers at its disposal to advance its objectives. Police powers are being used more frequently by governments to acquire property of all kinds.

One of the primary grounds upon which governments have increased their own authority to take private property is to advance the so-called war on drugs. Government seizure of private property without benefit of the Fifth Amendment's constitutional guarantee of just compensation for the property taken will be discussed separately in greater detail. The issue to be addressed at this juncture is whether the war on drugs is well conceived and designed to accomplish the objectives of public policy.

The war against drugs goes on and on, with no real hope of victory in the foreseeable future and barely any noticeable gains after tremendous exertion of government resources. American society remains the world's largest market for mind-altering drugs with detrimental, often fatal, side effects.

International criminal organizations battle each other and routinely kill anyone in the line of fire as they reap the tremendous profits available from the manufacture, distribution and sale of drugs. In the process, they spread terror and corruption in governments, including law enforcement, at all levels.

Drug users deplete their own resources, destroy their personal productivity, beg, borrow, steal, burglarize, rob, and sometimes kill to feed their drug habits, while traumatizing themselves and their families and friends. The human fallout fills our courts and prisons, severely impairing their performance of functions important to the success of a democratic society.

These destructive effects of drugs on society are well known. The question that needs answering is: why has public policy been so ineffective in fighting drug use and its accompanying antisocial activities? With billions of dollars already spent to do little better than maintain the status quo, public policy and its enforcement ought to be scrutinized for fundamental flaws.

From the viewpoint of formal statutory policy, federal and state governments assign the fight against drugs almost entirely to their criminal justice systems. Yet criminal law has obvious limitations in dealing with the objectives to be accomplished. Generally speaking, the objectives of public policy are to stop abuse of illegal drugs and rehabilitate the addicts; to dismantle the organizations which produce and distribute illegal drugs for profit; to curtail the activities of users who commit crimes to pay for their drug purchases; to stop the proliferation of guns on the streets used in the drug trade or purchased with drug profits; and, to ease the strain on the criminal (and civil) justice system caused by drug-related crime.

With relative certainty, we must conclude that not one of these objectives has been achieved, nor is a single one close to being well in hand. Even more alarming, we are not seeing substantial progress from the *status quo* on any one of these goals.

That is not to say nothing is being done. A great deal has to be done just to defend the barricades of civilization against the onslaught of the criminal drug industry. That industry pursues the estimated $150 Billion per year generated in the U.S. alone under the present system of drug control.

But if success in the war against drugs is to be defined as something more than marginal improvement at the edges of the continuing social disaster, government policy must be reassessed. This reassessment certainly should *not* be confined to debate of legalization of drug use as the only conceivable alternative to existing regulation through the criminal statutes.

In order to design a better public policy to achieve the goals already stated, a central truth must be confronted: profits are the mother's milk of the drug trade. As long as the tremendous profitability of illicit drugs survives, the drug dealers will find a way to serve the market.

Stiff criminal penalties have not been an effective deterrent even against drug use, and much less against drug dealing. Indeed, the more law enforcement succeeds in interdicting drug shipments and incarcerating the dealers and distributors, the higher goes the market price, and therefore, the profitability, of drugs on the street. Since profits are the driving force of the drug industry, and our public policy tends to increase profitability, clearly a change of policy is in order.

If public policy is redesigned to destroy the profitability of dealing in drugs, the dynamics of the drug problem will be changed fundamentally. Like cutting off the head of a snake, stripping the profits out of drugs would leave the international crime syndicates writhing and twisting, but with their ultimate demise almost equally a certainty. The profitability of drugs can be destroyed, at least the large scale, multi-billion dollar profitability that presently exists.

To do so requires designing and embracing a system to satisfy the market demand for drugs at low cost or no cost. This means legalizing the *use* of drugs *if obtained by the user from an authorized source*. At the same time, users should be required to register for counseling and rehabilitation.

By lowering the street price of drugs to 10% or less of their current cost, the profits flowing to the crime syndicates for use in terrorizing and corrupting the countries where production, manufacturing and distribution lines have reached will be reduced to near zero. This is public policy that can make a real difference in fighting the growth, power and pervasive influence of the drug culture.

Legalizing the *use* of drugs obtained from authorized outlets does *not* mean completely decriminalizing the regulation of presently illicit drugs. The penalties for illicit manufacture, distribution, sale *or use* of such drugs through unauthorized channels should be continued, perhaps even stiffened.

When dealers in drugs are no longer blinded by the dazzling glare of profits to be made—in other words, when the market conditions producing such profits no longer exist—criminal penalties should become much more persuasive to prospective adventurers that drug trafficking is an unattractive pursuit.

An understanding of acquisitivity adds little more than common sense to recognition of the fact that high profitability makes illegal drugs a very attractive activity. When profitability is removed, the attraction promptly fades and resources will no longer be fed into the treasuries of criminal enterprises.

Further study, understanding and appreciation of acquisitivity will provide an ever-improving template for testing the wisdom of many more public policies than can be examined here. Acquisitivity is a basic characteristic of human nature that provides the most efficient mechanism available for allocating resources for production of additional goods, services, knowledge and wealth. Acquisitivity feeds productivity, and productivity in turn feeds acquisitivity; neither can succeed without the other fulfilling its role.

Governments ought to interfere with this vital process considerably less frequently than is presently the case. Indeed, governments first ought to assure that they do nothing (or nothing more than absolutely necessary) to denigrate, disparage or disrupt the acquisitivity and productivity of individuals or business entities. That very significant review and reform of existing public policy should first be completed. Then the level of understanding of acquisitivity should have increased to the extent that consideration can be given to whether government may wisely take measures to encourage acquisitivity.

Seven

Acquisitivity And Property Rights

Each year, Americans remember and celebrate the Declaration of Independence of July 4, 1776. On that date, Thomas Jefferson, John Hancock, James Madison, Ben Franklin, John Adams and other Founding Fathers asserted that every person is endowed by their Creator with certain unalienable rights, and that among these are life, liberty and the pursuit of happiness.

After the ensuing long and difficult Revolutionary War for Independence, the people of America struggled even longer before deciding upon exactly what basis they were willing to give authority over them to any new central government. In 1789, the former colonies of Great Britain approved the Constitution of the United States of America as the foundation of a new republican democracy.

At the time of its adoption, the U.S. Constitution was a truly remarkable historical phenomenon. Those who drafted its provisions exhibited scholarship and rationality in designing the three branches to carry out the intended functions of government. The Framers displayed equally impressive statesmanship and diplomacy in balancing competing interests within the new government and among the member states.

But the fundamental objective of its design and the unprecedented achievement of the Constitution were the significant limits placed upon the powers of the new government. The government created was to have limited authority. Such an undertaking to restrain the power of government was formidable, since no successful example existed to emulate.

The Framers of the Constitution and the public at large were aware that their only means of restraining the new government were no more and no less than the paper, the pen and the words of the Constitution they wrote. No government in the history of the world, once in place, had been constrained other than by its own ideals or the power of its adversaries. The concept that a government's powers could be limited by a Constitution written and enacted by the governed people was the truly revolutionary contribution of American Independence. And so the Great Experiment in constitutional republican democracy was given its first breath and stirred to life.

Even when adopted, the constitutional assurances of limited government did not entirely satisfy a skeptical public. The people insisted upon the addition of a Bill of Rights spelling out specific ways in which the new government would not be permitted to act against them. James Madison drafted the Bill of Rights, which became the first ten amendments to the Constitution.

Of course, the Bill of Rights protects many more than ten rights. The First Amendment alone protects freedom of speech, assembly, press and religion. The Fifth Amendment alone protects a person against forced self-incrimination or double jeopardy for a criminal offense, and guarantees that the government cannot take a person's life, liberty or property without due process of law, or without just compensation for the property taken.

Imagine how different the American government and society would be today if the Bill of Rights had not been enacted. The importance of the instances in which one of those enumerated rights has been the only obstacle to government action against an individual is no less than awesome.

Yet, as when first conceived and ratified, the Constitution remains only words on paper, dependent entirely upon the knowledge and commitment of today's citizens to assure that its powers and constraints have real meaning. So how is the Great Experiment faring as the Millenium ends and the Twenty First Century begins? Are the citizens of today as skeptical of the "goodness" of unfettered government power and as jealous of their own rights and prerogatives as were the new Americans of 1789?

An affirmative answer to that question is nigh impossible. Politicians and schoolteachers often extol the virtues of the Constitution in concept, and some few actually cultivate an understanding of the provisions and policies that invigorate the document. In recent years Americans have heard the voices of commitment to limited government and renewal of American civilization. But when the chips are down in determining the role of the federal government in many important public issues, both the discourse and the decisions often seem divorced entirely from a foundation in Constitutional authority.

Consider, for example, the recent debate (or, more accurately, political struggle) about federal control of the use of electromagnetic broadcasting frequencies, otherwise known as the "airwaves." The airwaves are recurrently topical these days because new technology has developed the capability to transmit very high quality television pictures and sound in "digital" language by air or cable. The digital signal can be "compressed" to be much more compact than ordinary television broadcast signals. This compression of the signal creates room for about six times as many more television channels. In 1995, the existing television broadcasters wanted to be licensed to use the new space on the airwave spectrum as an adjunct of their existing broadcast rights. Of course, commercial television has become a major industry. Broadcast rights using new and improved technology become very valuable as they are put to commercial use.

The potential profits to be made in exploiting the new broadcast licenses made possible by digital technology caught the attention of officials of the federal government. One such official was then Senate Majority Leader and presumptive 1996 nominee of the Republican Party for President, Senator Bob Dole of Kansas. Senator Dole asserted during the course of the presidential primary season leading to the 1996 elections that issuing licenses to existing broadcasters for use of the newly created broadcasting capabilities would be "a giant corporate welfare program" and a giveaway of valuable assets belonging to the public. Instead of such a giveaway in breach of public trust, Senator Dole proposed that the broadcast rights for each portion of the airwave spectrum be auctioned to the highest bidder, and forecast that such an auction would raise no less than $70 Billion in much needed federal revenues.

Senator Dole was at that time a leading proponent of limited federal government and well known for his oft-repeated stump speech in which he reached into his left breast pocket and pulled out a copy of the Tenth Amendment to the Constitution. He then would recite the 29 words which reserve all powers not expressly granted to the federal government to the States or to the people, and would reiterate the fundamental importance of this provision in our approach to self-government. These days particularly, this is not an inconsiderable showing of *bona fides* in commitment to constitutional government.

Senator Dole was not alone in taking and defending his viewpoint regarding auctioning licenses to broadcast television signals as if electromagnetic frequencies were property owned by the federal government. No less a champion of the Constitution and individual liberty than Senator John McCain of Arizona asserted that the airwave spectrum "belongs to the taxpayers." Senator McCain termed the proposed statutory provision for issuing additional licenses to existing broadcasters without an auction "unconscionable."

Other respected members of the conservative political community weighed in as well, supporting the proposed auction to raise federal revenues. These supporters included the respected and influential Heritage Foundation, the *San Diego Union-Tribune* and *Reader's Digest.* What is wrong with this picture?

The problem is that the Constitution does not grant the federal government ownership of the "airwaves." The circumstance in 1995 and early 1996 that enabled the assertion of "public" ownership of the broadcast spectrum was the failure of the federal government as of that date to exercise properly its express authority under the Commerce Clause to regulate the use of the airwaves. The duty of Congress was and is to regulate the airwaves in such a manner as to enable communications and commercial exploitation in an orderly and efficient manner.

Despite the federal government's concerted efforts during the past 50 years to make it so, the power to regulate commerce is not yet synonymous with federal ownership of the business activity or property regulated. At least it is not synonymous until and unless American minds and courts can no longer distinguish the difference. Judging from the content of the debate on auctioning of broadcast rights, America may have arrived at that abysmal juncture.

During its 1995 Term, the Supreme Court of the United States surprised the governmental and legal communities by declaring a federal law invalid. The Court's ruling was all the more shocking because the statute was held to exceed the authority granted to Congress by the Commerce Clause of the Constitution to regulate commerce among the states.

The specific law held to be unconstitutional was one prohibiting possession of a gun within a specified distance from a public school. The Court simply could not see any vestige of interstate commerce involved in the conduct of possessing a gun at a certain location. Therefore, if that statute were deemed within the authority of the Commerce Clause, then no statute whatsoever could be regarded as outside the power of Congress to enact.

All in all, a pretty tepid performance of the Court's responsibility to uphold and defend the Constitution. But shocking in this day and age, nonetheless, because today many Americans readily assume unlimited federal power. As an adjunct of this fateful assumption, they have grown accustomed to getting nothing, rather than little, in the way of meaningful limits on government authority through their Supreme Court's decisions.

The Supreme Court's decision enforcing the scope of the Commerce Clause with respect to the gun control statute ought to be a useful reminder. The Commerce Clause is the primary underpinning of authority by the federal government over television broadcasting activities. Federal authority to regulate commerce such as broadcasting entails the power to license use so as to assure orderliness rather than chaos in the commerce involved. Promotion of increased commerce may likewise be a legitimate government objective of regulation.

But particularly when addressing commerce in the nature of communication of information, such as television, radio or telephone communications, other provisions of the Constitution, particularly the First Amendment, are importantly involved. The significant ancillary concerns for freedom of speech require that the proper role of the federal government in regulating the airwaves be limited strictly to the narrow function of efficient licensing to assure orderly use. This is far, far less a role for government than is entailed in the unsupportable contentions either that the federal government actually "owns" the airwaves, or that the federal government can withhold the airwaves from private use unless the prospective user will make a bargain and pay a price satisfactory to the government.

Even use of the term "airwaves" creates the misleading image of a thing or a piece of property that can be held and possessed by the government on behalf of the public. In actuality, the electromagnetic wave frequency spectrum is as much a part of the natural universe as are gravity, wind, light or air. The means to communicate by use of electromagnetic wave frequencies are products of scientific innovation, much as Thomas A. Edison invented the light bulb. And communication through the "airwaves" is still communication in the nature of speech by free people, perhaps one of the most important forms of it.

Undoubtedly the argument will be advanced, at least tacitly, that the "giveaway" of broadcast licenses was too high a price to pay for giving attention to a technicality under the Constitution. Seventy billion dollars is a lot of money, and the government could certainly have used the funds to do "good."

But surely, upon reflection, the alternative involves a much higher price—relinquishment of the inherited legacy of a government of limited powers. A government which can turn a delegated authority to regulate interstate commerce into the ownership of the essential means for conducting that commerce is a government which is unlikely to acknowledge or abide by any limits whatsoever.

The federal government is constitutionally empowered to collect a fee adequate to support the regulatory function before issuing a television broadcasting license. But the federal government is not empowered to withhold such a license until the potential user pays the economic value to be derived from exploiting the license. Unless that is the case, the Constitution will not protect any business from similar regulatory abuse under the Commerce Clause.

Why not auction licenses for airlines, for trains, for trucking, shipping, hospitals, physicians, lawyers or, indeed, any economic activity? If the Constitution doesn't protect the rights of everyone, including all potential users of the airwaves (not only existing broadcasters), it doesn't protect the rights of anyone.

The Telecommunications Act of 1996 resolved the issue of digital television broadcasting licenses by providing for "spectrum flexibility." This policy enables existing television broadcasters to use additional spectrum frequencies to broadcast high density television. However, that authorization is granted subject to the requirement that unused frequencies be relinquished to the government. Also, the statute reserves the potential for requiring payment of a winning bid at auction.

Of course, the Constitution does not require that licenses for new broadcasting frequencies be issued with any preference for existing broadcasters, except to the extent of their presently vested rights in current activities. All viable users should have an opportunity for the licenses. But its purely regulatory authority should not enable the federal government to leach the economic value out of the licensed commercial activity, simply because the activities are attractive to a large number of prospective licensees.

Rapidly advancing technologies affecting both television and radio broadcasting already enable vast amounts of information to be transmitted through wireless or cable infrastructure in "packets" without interference from other such packets transmitted simultaneously. These technological innovations and others to follow offer the prospect, if not the outright promise, of allowing unlimited numbers of broadcasters to operate without the need for specially licensed exclusive frequencies for each operator.

While auctioning of licenses would assure that only the broadcaster with the most money could operate, the new and improving technologies ought to increase the number of broadcasting licenses issued. At the same time, the necessity for any substantial governmental restrictions on the freedom of broadcasting activity ought to be reduced or eliminated entirely.

The airwaves auction debate is by no means the only example of current public discourse that treats the federal government as having slipped its moorings in the Constitution. Another instance is the treatment of so-called "civil forfeitures" of private assets.

Asset forfeitures presently result when a law enforcement agency, either federal, state or local, identifies a particular piece of property which has allegedly been used by some person (not necessarily the owner) in the perpetration of a crime. Special statutes have been enacted which authorize a law enforcement agency to show "probable cause" for believing the asset was used in a crime and then to seize the asset as government property. The private owner must sue to get the property back by proving that the asset was not used by anyone in committing a crime. Otherwise, the asset (a house, a farm, an office building, a car, a plane, a boat) belongs to the government and can be used or sold as the agency involved sees fit.

In the case of the U.S. federal government, and many individual state governments as well, the civil asset forfeiture laws are a burgeoning source of property ownership for government. As such, civil asset forfeiture laws are an assault upon private ownership rights in property, and thus upon individual initiative, innovation, acquisitivity and productivity.

Civil asset forfeiture did not originate with the Racketeer Influenced and Corrupt Organizations Act of 1972 (RICO), but RICO and the fight against organized crime gave birth to the widespread modern use of police powers to take private property without compensating for it. Since 1972, civil asset forfeiture powers have been given to government by more than 300 separate federal statutes, and innumerable state laws.

Many local police agencies, state police and highway patrols, as well as federal agencies, are presently confiscating private assets each year worth billions of dollars. These agencies responsible for public safety have a substantial financial incentive to seize assets, and a conflict of interest in doing so, since all or a significant portion of the seized assets will go directly to the agency itself for use in its operating budget.

One high official of a State highway patrol recently acknowledged (off the record) that the asset seizures by his agency had fallen sharply after the "politicians" had cut the agency's operating budget by a sum commensurate with the money received from sale of seized assets. His rationale for the drop in seizures: why do it if you can't get ahead?

Acquisitivity is as much a part of the human nature of persons running law enforcement and other government agencies as with any person managing a private business. The important difference is that law enforcement agencies have the force of law to assist their efforts. Beyond any reasonable doubt, the laws passed to aid seizure of private assets are subject to flagrant abuse. A candid assessment of the records of the rising multitude of asset seizures would likely prove that such seizures have produced many more seriously damaged, innocent victims than punished criminals.

The innocent Michigan woman whose dilapidated family car was lost to seizure by police because her husband used the car to solicit a prostitute is only the very smallest tip of the asset seizure iceberg. The U.S. Supreme Court allowed the family car to be taken despite her conceded innocence of any involvement in the crime. Much more substantial assets are often seized for arguably minor offenses, such as a family home taken for the offense of a few ounces of marijuana found in a car garaged there.

Forbes magazine on May 20, 1996, reported that a Florida real estate developer paid $8.6 Million to the federal government as a settlement after two years of litigation. The $8.6 Million was paid by the developer to recover his properties seized upon an allegation that one of his business associates had violated federal export laws (without the knowledge of the developer).

An innocent citizen who desires an effective fight against crime may be tempted to justify such government activity as the deserved rewards of criminal conduct. But the true test of a just law is whether the law withstands the fairness test when that innocent citizen is himself the object of the law's effect. Asset seizures are occurring daily that would not pass this test in the judgment of any reasonable person. Even one such occurrence ought to be unthinkable in the United States of America.

Nevertheless, the momentum of government action to seize private assets is increasing. First used in drug-related crime, then spreading into general crime such as prostitution/solicitation, asset forfeiture more recently is moving into economic activity such as environmental regulation. Why? Because, in simplest terms, as always, *the government wants the money.* The critical ingredient for such governmental misconduct is already in place—the Supreme Court of the United States does not have the fortitude to stop it.

The Supreme Court has the means (and, indeed, the Constitutional duty) to stop such asset seizures in their tracks. The Takings Clause of the Fifth Amendment strictly prohibits the federal government from taking property belonging to any person unless the property is needed for public use and just compensation is paid to the person deprived of the property. This, of course, is a most important, fundamental limit upon government power and a crucial protection of an individual's human rights.

It is no exaggeration to assert that, in the most profound sense, the Takings Clause is the key constitutional safeguard that prevents the government from making every person a ward of the state. If a government can take a person's property without paying full value for it, then that person must ultimately depend upon the state for sustenance and has no independent means to assure self-sufficiency for himself or his family. Thus, the Takings Clause is the defining distinction between the all-powerful state and the state that is controlled by those governed.

How poignant that Americans in the year 2000 are so badly in need of a lesson in the fundamental importance of the Takings Clause protection of the human right to acquire and possess property. That was the first and foremost right (other than life and liberty) stated in the

Virginia Declaration of Rights of June 12, 1776, which so greatly influenced Jefferson in drafting the Declaration of Independence and
Madison in drafting the Bill of Rights. The lesson is, however, needed
badly. Every American stands close upon the precipice of losing that
right due to the onslaught of government power dressed in the benev-
olent guise of the "public interest."

Yet Americans need look no farther than their southern border to see
a modern example of a long established civilization without a Takings
Clause. Mexico's national constitution contains what might be termed
the socialist's antithesis of the Takings Clause—a governmental guarantee that every peasant will be given free land.

As so often occurs in central planning with good intentions, unintended consequences overwhelm the anticipated benefits. The Mexican
promise of land to peasants causes every landowner to be insecure in
his property, lest it be taken by the government for giving to others. As
a result, landowners do not invest new capital in their own country.
Capital flight to the north and elsewhere robs the Mexican economy of
vitality and growth.

Where does this leave the intended benefactor of the "free land"
guarantee, the peasant? Crawling across Mexico's northern border at
night. Trying to avoid the search lights of an unsympathetic border
patrol. Striving to enter an economic "paradise," where the unbenevolent
Takings Clause of the Fifth Amendment provides the private property
foundation of economic wealth for the largest middle class in the history
of the world. Hoping to become a participant in an unmatched
prosperity accomplished within barely more than 200 years, following
millennia of relatively unremarkable economic progress.

The protection of a person's rights in his property was a primary
objective of the Framers of the Constitution. Thomas Jefferson's first
draft of the Declaration of Independence stated the unalienable rights
of man to "life, liberty and the pursuit of *property*"—later editing after

review by Benjamin Franklin and John Adams restated property as the more generic objective of "happiness."

For students of human nature, as James Madison certainly was, the protection of political freedom is another means of protecting rights in property. Madison was quite aware that the political freedoms of speech, press and assembly are most likely to be put to use by individuals seeking to advance economic rights centered upon ownership of property.

After all, of what real utility is the political right to speak freely about governmental affairs if the government has the power to take your property whenever the government or "public" interest is arguably served by doing so? And of what use is the "due process of law" if it means only that you are entitled to a public hearing before the government takes your property for a purpose deemed appropriate by the Congress or other legislature? The answer to both questions is not much use at all. Yet that is, in general terms, where our constitutional rights stand today under the decisions of the Supreme Court.

During the 1930's, President Franklin D. Roosevelt threatened to "pack the Court" by appointing additional members unless the Supreme Court discontinued its rulings holding various "New Deal" legislation to be unconstitutional. Under the pressure of this threat from the Executive Branch, the Supreme Court abandoned its long-held view that "substantive due process" entitles a person to a determination of fundamental fairness in the law which authorizes his private property to be taken. Since that watershed event, the Court has ruled that the "due process of law" guaranteed by the Fifth Amendment requires only two things: (i) a public hearing before the property is taken, and (ii) a determination by the court that the statute authorizing the taking of property has a rational purpose in the view of the legislature which enacted the statute. Obviously, this brand of due process is flimsy protection against any government wanting property.

A reasonable person might believe that due process of law also requires that the Takings Clause of the Fifth Amendment be enforced at the public hearing. But the Supreme Court has gone to considerable lengths to avoid the subject of the Takings Clause whenever possible.

If the subject is unavoidable, the Court has sometimes written vigorously, even stating that personal rights in property deserve the same degree of protection under the Constitution as political rights under the First Amendment. For example, "property doesn't have rights—people do." Nevertheless, the undeniable fact is that the Court imposes much stricter scrutiny upon a statute infringing First Amendment "political" or "religious" rights than the Court imposes with respect to a statute which infringes a person's rights in his property.

Never has this been more apparent in a public forum outside the Court itself than in the Hearing Room of the United States Senate as the Chairman of the Judiciary Committee began the questioning of Circuit Judge Clarence Thomas as a nominee to the Supreme Court. Long before Professor Anita Hill made her appearance at the hearing, Chairman Joseph Biden of Delaware stated what he described to Judge Thomas as "the most important question you will be asked at these hearings."

Chairman Biden first described the high degree of "strict scrutiny" exercised by the Court in reviewing state or federal statutes which are challenged as infringements of rights protected by the First Amendment. Senator Biden next described the reduced level of scrutiny applied by the Supreme Court when a statute infringing rights in property is under review. Senator Biden then expressly warned Judge Thomas with words to the effect that "if you give the wrong answer to my question, I will do everything within my power to see that you never sit on the Supreme Court."

The Chairman's question was: "Do you agree with the Court's existing decisions giving higher scrutiny to the protection of First Amendment rights than to the protection of rights in property?" Judge

Thomas answered with words to the effect: "Mr. Chairman, I have no problem with the existing decisions of the Court on those issues."

No subtlety at all was apparent or intended in the blunt message from the Chairman of the Senate Judiciary Committee, who impliedly spoke for the Senate. If you wish to be confirmed by the United States Senate as a Justice of the U.S. Supreme Court, you must promise to stay out of the Congress' way when we want to take private property.

Unfortunately, the Court fully complies with this Senatorial demand in substantially all significant cases. Sometimes the Court accepts review of a Takings Clause case involving state or local government infringement of property rights, usually in real estate. The Court then states the limits of government authority, but in vague and ambiguous terms, thereby enabling the state or local government agency to run circles around the private person attempting to get compensation for his lost property rights in the lower courts.

Possibly the worst examples of such experiences occur in California cases. A frequently quoted observation on these circumstances is that a person considering a lawsuit to obtain compensation for property taken by the government would do better to slit his wrists, because doing so will achieve the same result in a much faster and less expensive way than filing suit.

The Supreme Court's preference for avoiding Takings Clause issues often gives rise to important dislocations in the law, and sometimes to downright irony. Such a circumstance occurred recently in the Court's 1996 opinion overturning a punitive damages award made by an Alabama jury. An Alabama physician had purchased a new German-made BMW, but later learned that the car's paint had been touched-up after being damaged during shipping. For this misconduct, the doctor was awarded compensatory damages covering all economic losses in the amount of about $6,000. But to punish the misconduct of the car manufacturer, the jury awarded the doctor an additional $2 Million in punitive damages.

Of course, when a jury and a court takes property from one private party and transfers it to another private party, the transfer is made through use of government power. Therefore, a reasonable person might think that the Takings Clause's prohibition against government taking of property without just compensation might place a limit on such government activity. Indeed, decisions under the Takings Clause have held that the government is not permitted to take property for the private use of another person under any circumstance—even if compensation is paid for the property taken.

Notwithstanding the important policies expressed in the Takings Clause intending to prevent this sort of government action favoring one party and disfavoring another by transferring wealth between them, the Supreme Court accepted review of the punitive damages case—not under the Takings Clause, but under the Due Process Clause. Review of the case under the Takings Clause would have undoubtedly produced, in at least a majority of the minds on the Court, too rigid a result. Either the Takings Clause would prohibit punitive damages altogether, as it should, or would not inhibit the award of punitive damages at all, if found to be inapplicable. So the Court reviewed the punitive damages award only under the Due Process Clause.

Now, however, the great irony of the Court's conduct becomes apparent. In order to overturn the punitive damages award as "grossly unfair" in proportion to the misconduct involved, the Court implicitly and necessarily resurrected "substantive due process"—the testing of government action for fundamental fairness in the eye of the Court. That legal doctrine, as already mentioned, was intellectually discredited and interred in the 1930's when President Franklin Roosevelt threatened to pack the Court with additional members. The dissenting opinion of Justice Scalia in the BMW case notes that substantive due process cannot provide a proper foundation for the 5-4 split decision of the Court. Yet no Justice suggested that the Takings Clause should have been the correct restriction against the gross transfers of property between citizens by government outside the bounds of compensation for damages suffered.

The Takings Clause is effectively disfavored by the Supreme Court primarily because the Takings Clause is so disfavored by the Congress. As the head of the Judicial Branch of the federal government, the Supreme Court is dependent upon the Congress for its financial resources as well as other legislative cooperation.

Still, at least a portion of the disfavor shed upon the Takings Clause by the Court emanates from the Court's own instincts as an arm of government. The Court enjoys the power of authority to transfer property between parties if it chooses to do so, for much the same reason as most politicians or other government personnel.

A common human instinct appears to abhor power in others, while admiring and coveting power in one's self. This instinct is apparent not only in Justices of the Supreme Court, but throughout the federal and state judiciaries. Consider, for example, the members of the jury in the BMW case recently decided in the Alabama state court and reviewed by the Supreme Court. Would a jury member prefer to be instructed by the court that his authority is limited by the Takings Clause to awarding the complaining doctor no more than the damages sufficient to compensate for his actual losses (about $6,000)? Or, would the jury member prefer to be authorized to give one party $2 Million of the other party's money if he chooses to do so? Clearly, the jury member will choose to have the power, regardless of whether the power is used in a particular case. So will the judge of the trial court, and so will the judges of the appellate courts, and so do the Justices of the Supreme Court of the United States.

That the Supreme Court may be the crucial flaw in the hopes of Americans for enforcement and preservation of the human rights expressed in the Constitution would come as no surprise to the Framers. Alexander Hamilton writing as Publius in *The Federalist No. 78* concedes that standing against majority opinion as faithful guardians of the Constitution "would require an uncommon portion of fortitude in the judges to do their duty." This contemporaneous expression of concern for the fortitude of judges is now being sorely tested as a well-entrenched federal government moves through its third century under the Constitution.

Judges are by no means solely responsible for preserving the constitutional rights of Americans. The President and every member of each house of Congress takes a solemn oath to uphold and defend the Constitution. Yet so many in every political station continue to pursue the interests (of "factions" as Madison called them) which inexorably increase government power, cutting the chains that were intended to bind and restrict the government, while at the same time trampling individual rights in the name of the "public interest."

Political leaders are not alone in being charged with safeguarding the rights enunciated by the Constitution. Those rights and perhaps others were proclaimed by Jefferson and the brave souls who signed the Declaration on July 4, 1776, to be unalienable and endowed in each person by his Creator. Each person who aspires to claim and advance these unalienable rights must know, understand and appreciate their nature and content. Only then will the extent of the task of upholding and defending the Constitution become fully apparent.

The requirements of Constitutional limits upon government and protection of individual rights have not been fully considered by those who assert the "public" ownership of rights to communicate through the airwaves. The government might just as easily have asserted ownership of the light and the darkness, so that Thomas Edison could not make use of his light bulb invention until he first became the highest bidder at an auction for a license to light a room.

The direct positive or adverse implications of the governmental treatment of television broadcast rights will be tremendously important for the telecommunications industry and for our society. But the impact of that government action upon constitutional rights essential for the free exercise of acquisitivity and productivity is far more significant.

The Commerce Clause granting Congress the authority to regulate commerce among the States does not mean that Congress effectively "owns" the right of any person to do business, or that the government may "auction" that right to the highest bidder. Otherwise, the battle to maintain limited government power that began with ratification of the Constitution has been lost in the fullest and most complete sense. All that would remain in that dreadful eventuality would be the "mop-up operation" whereby government consolidates its victory over the Constitution. The Framers' hopes for limiting the role of the state in our lives would be ended in defeat.

Discussion of the role of certain Republicans in promoting the premise that the federal government owns the proprietary interest in use of broadcast frequencies is by no means intended to suggest that Republicans are the sole cause or even the primary cause of that constitutional concern. To the contrary, Republican leadership in the House of Representatives had been proceeding at the time to authorize the issuance of high density television broadcast licenses without an auction. Senator Dole may have been motivated to act as he did in order to blunt expected criticism from his Democrat opposition in the Congress and in the upcoming 1996 Presidential campaign. The Telecommunications Act of 1996 providing for issuance of licenses without an auction to the highest bidder was enacted with Republican leadership and support in both houses of Congress.

Far from asserting the constitutional concerns raised by the governmental claim of ownership of electromagnetic communications capabilities, the Democrats have been far ahead of the Republicans in racing to gain the additional spending money raised in auctions of rights to utilize cellular telephone broadcast frequencies. In fact, such auctions have already been conducted by the Federal Communications Commission, with single companies actually submitting multi-billion dollar bids (and at least one bidder defaulting in payment of the bid amount).

The left wing of the political spectrum has contributed to the preservation and expansion of political or civil rights under the Constitution, but the left has also added importantly to the growth of government power in economic regulation and social welfare. Some of the growth in the power of the state in police power and military defense may be fairly attributed to the influences of so-called conservatives. But liberals have unhesitatingly spurred taxing and spending programs of the federal government during the past forty years to extremes that would have been condemned from all parts of the polity any time in earlier American history.

Where is the last ditch, all-out opposition from the American Civil Liberties Union or from the Freedom Foundation to the assertion that the U.S. Government owns all rights to communicate through the airwaves? The relative silence on this monumentally significant public policy issue is nothing less than astonishing when so much energy has been devoted in past years to such concerns as parades in Skokie and crucifixes on public lawns.

Each enumerated Constitutional right and every unalienable human right endowed in each person are priceless and invaluable. Seventy billion dollars is, indeed, a lot of money and the auction of television broadcast licenses is tempting. The existing large broadcasting companies would certainly pay the amounts necessary to retain their franchises. After all, they have the resources, and such a high price discourages smaller competition.

But the price already paid to purchase and preserve the Constitution includes the lives lost in the Revolutionary War, the Civil War, World War II and every other intervening war or "conflict." In each of those trials, the constitutionally protected human rights of Americans were in peril and might have been lost, except for the efforts and sacrifices of those who stepped into the breach to preserve them. No, $70 Billion is not enough money for the loss of any Constitutional right; not twice that nor ten times that amount.

This time all Americans, as individuals, are the ones called upon to rise to the challenge. The Constitution will not be preserved by repeating hollow words on Independence Day. The Constitution will be preserved only by honoring and abiding by its principles and policies, in word and in deed, in each and every instance where government would prefer to ignore it.

This includes instances where a "majority" of the public would prefer government action against a less influential minority interest group. This includes even those instances in which the resulting government policy is harder to explain in a stump speech or in a campaign ad. All this is possible when each person understands his rights in their full context and strives to protect them for himself and for others.

When public policies enforced by governments weaken the rights of individuals in private property, those public policies run counter to the natural mechanism that centers upon acquisitivity. Weakened rights in private property mean less value in that property and, therefore, lower incentive to acquire it.

When any government, whether local, state or federal, acts to extract value from property, whether by taxation or regulation, the hurdle to be overcome by the natural mechanism for resource allocation becomes more difficult. In the very practical environment affecting each individual or entity, acquisitivity must find resources of sufficient value to feed productivity. In return, productivity must replenish acquisitivity with resources of equal or greater value. Otherwise the productive process will fail. Government ought to obstruct and burden this process as little as possible.

In every instance of government action to broaden its own powers at the expense of private rights in property, the capacity of acquisitivity to fulfill its role in fostering productivity is undercut. Communist ideology enforced by government power stifled acquisitivity throughout

Russia and the Soviet empire for 70 years quite effectively, and productivity of the subjugated people was set back immensely.

Western governments should learn through this example. Making the same mistakes, but smaller ones with less extreme interference in personal acquisitivity, is not the ideal pattern to be followed by democratic governments. Yet incremental assaults intended to cut back private rights of ownership, often rationalized by the greater wealth produced by those very rights, have been the experience in America and in Europe for generations.

The premise of many Western politicians seems to be "some in society are so wealthy, we can afford to cut back on their rights, and we ought to do so as a matter of moral principle." That premise should be reconsidered. Acquisitivity as a natural mechanism for resource allocation may be mankind's best hope for economic growth and for long term survival of the species. Politicians seeking to do good should first assure they do no harm.

Eight

Acquisitivity.com

Communication of information is an elemental concern of life. This has been so since the origin of all life, certainly animal life, and more fundamentally so since the onset of humankind. Whether developing the skills and knowledge of hunting or gathering, or deciding between fight or flight, the timely receipt of information from independent sources has been critical to the success of every species, and particularly humans.

Communications affect every aspect of life. Parental care, family relations, learning, working, social relations, public policy, saving, consuming, investing. Name any subject of interest to you, and consider how importantly it is reliant upon and impacted by the efficiency of communications. The same has been said in many more eloquent ways about individuals. How well a person communicates, both in sending and in receiving information, will largely determine success or failure in the various endeavors of life.

A significant hallmark of our current age is that communications of certain types are becoming much faster and much cheaper. This is already having a profoundly beneficial effect upon millions of people around the world, and will ultimately change the courses of billions of lives.

Of course, communications at a personal level cannot be replaced or substituted by new technologies. The love in a mother's eye, a father's guidance and encouragement of his child, the development of trust and binding commitment between husband and wife, the nurturing of lasting bonds between friends, are personal communications that must be performed by individuals. They will continue to be dependent upon personal principles of conduct involving ideas of morality, right and wrong, and spiritual beliefs.

But even these areas of deeply personal relationships will be subject to, and benefited by, the ongoing advances in communications technology. They will be affected because each individual will have greatly increased access to information that may benefit his handling of personal affairs. Each individual will have relatively fast and cheap access to information affecting his education, his work, his hobbies, his politics, and any other vestige of his curiosity. This will provide the opportunities for vastly improved decision-making and conduct.

Imagine a mother who better understands her infant's needs and conduct, and who can quickly obtain reliable information about perceived symptoms and responsive care. Such a mother may be able to feel and convey her love and care for her child even more effectively than the most adoring parent of the Elizabethan era.

The aids to everyday living concerns offered by improved technologies do not threaten to turn life's personal relations into artificial celluloid. Put to its natural and rational uses, improved communications technology will be widely embraced and welcomed for its beneficial effects on personal life.

The British historian Paul Johnson has chronicled in insightful and persevering detail the previously unparalleled advances in the conditions of civilization made during the 15 years of relative peace following the defeat of Napoleon at Waterloo in 1815.[43] The Twentieth

Century, despite the two World Wars and numerous military conflicts, will be regarded as an even more prolonged period of tremendously dynamic technological progress. Each of these two eras has been marked by noticeably rising living conditions for many millions of people around the world.

That is why ordinary people can be enthusiastic and even comfortable in welcoming the changes that technological innovation will bring to their lives. No one need be shocked by being afforded the advantages of improved capabilities that did not exist a few short years ago.

A person living at the end of the Twentieth Century and the beginning of the Twenty First need not necessarily think, respond or change faster than another person who lived during the Roaring Twenties or during the Depression of 1930's America. Today's individual has the capability to obtain information relevant to personal and business decisions much more quickly and cheaply, with much less work, than was the case in earlier times. What earlier inhabitant of the planet would not have preferred that circumstance?

No, today's infrastructure for rapid and cheap communication of information is not a harbinger of shocking change. It is a tool of exquisite delight for the energetic person seeking to advance his interests. This is so because time and money are saved in abundance as compared to the old ways of gathering information. A person without such interests, if one exists, may use the communications capabilities for entertainment or diversion, or may ignore them completely.

Fears harbored for an extended period of time may cause a condition of "shock" that inhibits a person's normal responses. A person who experiences fear at a particular turn of events may be responding rationally or irrationally, depending upon how a reasonable, rational person would assess the same events.

The advent of faster, cheaper, more efficient communications is not rationally viewed as fearsome. A clear and objective view of the advent of improved communications is important at the outset in order that ordinary individuals will not be persuaded they are about to experience fearsome, detrimental changes in their lives.

From present indications, ordinary people will greet the improvements in communications warmly and use them to their greatest advantage. There is little reason to experience future shock simply because communications are faster and cheaper and, accordingly, information is easier to access.

After all, what is so fearsome or hard to accept about cheaper rates for long distance telephone calls? For millions of Americans, Europeans, Canadians, Australians, South and Central Americans and Asians, using a personal computer to gain access to the internet is already a daily activity. For those individuals and many others joining them each day, the prospect of making a free long distance telephone call by clicking the mouse connected to their PC monitor screen will seem to be a completely natural and foreseeable extension of their past experiences.

Technology called Voice Over Internet Protocol (VoIP) already enables transmittal of telephone calls at such low cost that free long distance (domestic) calls are being offered to assist the sale of products, advertising and other services. This, of course, is only one aspect of the current progress in communications.

After enactment of the Tax Reform Act of 1986 by the U.S. Congress eliminated some "progressive" tax brackets and reduced marginal tax rates, other governments around the world followed suit in a wave of tax reform. This occurred for two primary reasons. First, each government had to protect its own economy against flight of capital to the friendlier American tax system. And, secondly, other governments became persuaded of the economic merits of the reforms, much as the U.S. Congress had been.

Now largely the same wave of deregulation by other governments is occurring in the wake of the enactment of the Telecommunications Act of 1996 by the U.S. Congress. Much of the acceleration of progress in communications technology and services is occurring as a result of governmental deregulation of the field. Government grants of monopoly status to domestic telephone companies are being moderated or removed by various countries around the world in order to gain the advantages of private investments in new communications infrastructure using improved technologies.

These events will enable increased competition and dramatically lower rates of charges for international communications services. The benefits are already flowing to individuals and businesses alike, and the results are predictable. One such result is higher investment in new communications infrastructure, both domestically and internationally. Also, volumes of traffic in voice and data are growing at explosive rates. The communications progress being experienced today will become even more apparent in the months and years ahead.

Why so much attention to communications when the subject is acquisitivity? Because, as in so many other aspects of life, communications are so fundamentally important in the exercise of human acquisitivity. The dramatic improvements in speed and cost of communications will have a profoundly significant impact upon the capabilities of individuals to acquire, to produce and to consume.

This impact is already becoming apparent within the context of the synergistic, mutual support among different segments of related industries. Progress in the technologies of transmission media such as cable, optical fiber and wireless have important effects spurring investment and progress in development of routers and switching devices, as well as personal computers, servers, data storage and software. Each innovation in a particular field provides a platform for several advances in related technologies.

To the outside observer, the technology scene may appear to be a chaotic frenzy. The best efforts of the financial markets to track and rationalize technological developments have been largely successful to the extent that financing of promising technologies has been relatively plentiful. But the financial press, particularly that reporting to the general public through the mainstream media, often fails to comprehend or communicate the importance of particular new innovations. When that occurs, the public can only view the financial markets as frenzied, and the rationality of the markets suffers as a consequence.

Market information is one of the areas where the communications revolution is already making a significant difference. The higher speed and lower cost of communications are allowing many individual investors, as well as money management professionals, much broader access to detailed information relevant to investments.

This is so much the reality of the current financial markets that few investors at any level rely upon the media any longer for information to guide their investment decisions. The general media may be a considerable factor in carrying information to a broader audience. But many investors will have completed their due diligence in analyzing the implications of company actions by using access to electronic sources freely available through the internet or through proprietary data services before the financial media reports the story.

As communications become faster and cheaper, every aspect of business enterprise will be affected. Even now, businesses large and small are being overhauled to identify each detail that can be handled more efficiently through use of the new electronic tools being designed and introduced by technological entrepreneurs.

E-commerce is already affecting dramatically the manner and means by which businesses do business with each other. Almost every business relies upon supplies, parts and services from many other companies in order to produce the goods and services eventually sold to its own customers. Since so many businesses already use computers and communications within the company, adaptation of that capability to the business to business commerce application has been both logical and predictable, although the phenomenal growth has been described as entirely unforeseen.

As communications are crucially important in all aspects of life, the same is true of all aspects of business. The manner of meeting each communications need of every business is presently being addressed based on the new parameters of increased speed and reduced costs. This reassessment of the mechanics of communications is producing the wholesale redesign of many business organizations in a tremendously dynamic environment that will be ongoing for the foreseeable future. No doubt the ingenuity of countless human minds will be devoted to identifying and exploiting every means by which acquisitivity and productivity can be benefited by faster, cheaper communications.

Businesses have now taken the lead in exploiting the benefits of the communications revolution because, in a manner of speaking, their business depends upon it. Businesses ordinarily are organized and staffed to address such consequential concerns. But individuals are not exempted from the necessity of similar rethinking and reorganization of their personal endeavors if they are to be as successful as they are capable of being in the new communications age.

Faster and cheaper communication sounds like a relatively straightforward set of factors that will simply enable purchase and use of more of the same. However, when speed and cost are each dramatically changed, the implications are more far-reaching.

The improvements in communications infrastructure presently being brought into use will enable individuals and businesses to obtain and utilize more and better information. More and better information will be obtained because the higher speed and lower cost of communications will enable a broader, more thorough search for relevant data to be made than would otherwise have been the case. The predictable outcome of this circumstance is that more and better information will be the foundation for better decision-making. This ought to result in more successful acquisitivity and higher rates of growth for the production of goods, services and wealth.

Evidence is readily apparent that this process is well underway. The historically long and relatively strong economic growth experienced in the United States during the 1980's and 1990's has been fed largely by the even stronger growth of technology industries.

These industries include computer equipment and peripherals, computer software and, more recently, telecommunications, and the construction of plants and infrastructure for those industries. Without these powerful components, the economic picture of the United States during the late Twentieth Century would be starkly different. Each of these industries is now being nourished by the others through synergistic relations that appear increasingly compelling.

Again the point is well worth emphasis that this exceptional economic growth is occurring in industries that are minimally regulated by the federal government or, as in the case of the telecommunications industry, have been significantly deregulated in recent years. One can hardly imagine the likelihood or even the possibility of comparably dynamic innovation occurring in any industry where government regulation maintains comprehensive control.

Consider, by contrast, the health care industry. Described as comprising one seventh of the entire U.S. economy, the industry that delivers medical services and medicines through physicians and hospitals to the American public is significantly regulated and, thus, controlled at every level by government. This is the present reality despite the well-publicized failure of the Clinton administration to succeed in gaining enactment of legislation in 1994 that would have largely federalized control of health care.

The federal government regulates much of the health care in the U.S. because federal programs pay for the services, and also because individuals and interest groups often complain to politicians and legislators about health care services. No prescription medicine is permitted to be prescribed or sold for the treatment of humans without extensive prior testing and approval by the federal Food and Drug Administration. The

FDA approval, although "streamlined" in recent years to speed the advance of new medicines to market, still requires years and millions of dollars for approval of each drug.

State governments regulate health care even more closely through the licensing of physicians and certification of hospitals, the licensing of pharmacies and testing laboratories, and similar oversight of other health care facilities. State agencies now commonly exercise close scrutiny of every detail of a health care organization's operations. This regulatory control certainly governs conduct directly connected to the ministering of health care. In addition, regulation often covers all financial practices as well, such as pricing and billing, and even reaches into evaluation of accounts receivable and whether unpaid bills should be written off.

Whether this government regulation is ultimately beneficial to the people is fairly debatable. But the fact that responding to government regulatory oversight requires very substantial time and resources of health care organizations is beyond dispute.

The adverse consequences for dynamic innovation in an industry characterized by a close regulatory environment should come as no surprise. Consider the experience in recent years with the advent of Health Maintenance Organizations (HMO's) in the U.S. health care industry. Responding primarily to the problem of extraordinarily high rates of inflation in health care costs that arose during the late 1970's and 1980's, HMO's addressed that issue quite effectively. As a result, participation in HMO programs grew dramatically and HMO's prospered financially.

One of the significant advantages HMO's had at their outset was the legal protection that a dissatisfied participant could not bring suit for more than payment of the proper amounts of the HMO plan of benefits. This statutory policy was based upon the premise that if an HMO was required to pay any more than proper plan benefits to any participant, the HMO's resources to pay benefits to all other participants would be reduced accordingly.

However, even as HMO's offered lower premium rates for full health care, some participants complained that the quality of care received was deficient. Eventually the lobbying of Congress by dissatisfied participants of HMO's, and by the organizations of trial lawyers seeking to represent the participants' interests, persuaded Congress to amend the law. Now federal law permits HMO's to be sued for consequential damages in addition to plan benefits, though with a maximum limit on the amount of such damages that can be awarded.

Almost before the ink was dry on the President's signature of the new law, law firms specializing in class action litigation began announcing the filing of suits seeking to represent thousands of allegedly aggrieved participants in a single action against their HMO. Such class actions will try to prove objectionable HMO policies affecting many participants in damaging ways. If they are successful, the result will drain substantial financial resources from the defendant HMO's.

Apart from the amendment of federal law to allow HMO's to be sued for consequential damages, the government had already begun to pinch and pressure HMO finances from a different perspective. The HMO's had organized themselves initially to deliver health care services profitably based on then existing government programs. When the government noticed that HMO's were actually prospering with the government payments as they were, the government reduced the level of payments significantly.

The immediate result was the transformation of the HMO industry from a condition of financial prosperity to one of financial weakness. Some HMO's announced they could no longer accept participants covered by the government programs. In the late 1990's, individual HMO's actually began declaring bankruptcy in escalating numbers. Not surprisingly, as HMO's have weakened, health care cost inflation has begun rising again.

Arguably, much of the inflation experienced in health care costs may be charged to the influences of government programs, money and regulation. The taxpayers of governments, both federal and state, have been hit very hard by the rising costs of health care pushing program budgets ever higher. In those circumstances, it seems particularly ironic that the HMO industry created to address and solve the problem of rampant inflation in health care costs may meet its demise indirectly at the hands of government.

The HMO experience is but one of the more apparent fields in which the role of government may be counterproductive to innovation and problem solving. Without leaving the health care industry, the problems facing approximately one quarter of the U.S. population who seek health care without the benefit of insured or prepaid coverage are instructive.

The premiums for most insured and prepaid health care plans are paid by employers as business expenses. Therefore, the premiums are pre-tax dollars so far as the covered participant who benefits from the plan is concerned.

For the uninsured person, by contrast, any health care purchased is paid with after-tax dollars. That is a very significant financial penalty for the uninsured, imposed by government policy.

But this is only the beginning of the problems of the uninsured. Essentially all insured or prepaid groups negotiate with health care providers to obtain acceptable contract prices for the services to be purchased. Individual uninsured patients, on the other hand, are not organized to negotiate for comparable savings in the fees and charges to be paid for the care they receive.

Consequently, the uninsured patient, or "cash customer," is charged and billed the highest prices charged by the health care provider. These prices are known as the "usual and customary" rates, and are often as high as several multiples of the amounts charged to groups at negotiated rates. Thus, the patient least able to afford the services is charged by far the highest amount by the health care providers.

This shameful reality is made even more harsh for the uninsured by the fact that the providers have an incentive to charge higher prices to the uninsured. The providers report these high billing rates to various government programs. In so doing, the high billing rates charged to the uninsured become leverage in the health care provider's efforts to persuade the government to pay higher rates for services to other patients covered by the government programs.

The State of California adds yet a further ironic twist to the mistreatment of its uninsured population. California law places strict licensing requirements on all health care plans operating in the State. A health care plan is defined by State law as including any entity that receives an advance payment in connection with arranging the delivery of health care services.

The California licensing procedure requires the applicant to pay fees covering the costs of reviewing the extensive application. Also, the applicant must pay per capita fees annually based on membership. In addition, the license requires substantial financial deposits with the State Department of Corporations and even more substantial financial reserves within the licensed health care plan itself. Finally, and perhaps most significantly, California licensing requires that the health plan licensee accept responsibility (and liability) for the quality of health care delivered by the providers serving the plan membership.

These licensing requirements may sound perfectly reasonable for an entirely prepaid health care plan such as an HMO. The HMO members (or their employers) are advancing the payment to the HMO of premiums to be used for providing all health care services needed by the membership during a future time interval. In those circumstances, appropriate safeguards ought to be in place to assure that the HMO's financial reserves will be adequate to pay for those future promised benefits.

However, California's Department of Corporations has interpreted its licensing powers as covering even a plan that simply seeks to negotiate better prices from health care providers for the uninsured. Since this network for the uninsured would charge a small membership fee in exchange for negotiating prices comparable to the significant discounts in charges obtained by most prepaid or insured groups, the State insists that the uninsured network plan must be licensed. Which essentially means the network for the uninsured must be insured.

When advised that the uninsured cannot afford insurance, which is why they are uninsured in the great majority of instances, the State of California says that is regrettable but the law leaves no choice. So the uninsured of California continue to pay by far the highest charges for health care of any consumers, and the State refuses to allow a network to negotiate lower prices on their behalf unless the network is licensed in the same manner as an HMO.

This regulatory outcome illustrates how government intervention often produces a result both adverse to business innovation and at least arguably inimical to the public interest. A larger lesson, however, is that private innovation will not occur when government control stifles it. Those individuals who succeed in innovating on an historic scale are ones fortunate or wise enough to have chosen fields of activity where government regulation did not predetermine an adverse outcome.

With the startling successes of computer technology, the internet and communications to serve as the patterns and the motivation for emulation, public policy makers should undertake to create more "innovation zones" relatively free of regulatory controls. Innovation Zones would not be geographical zones, but fields of personal and business activity, where government intercedes in decision-making as little as possible.

Deregulation of industries such as transportation got a foothold in the 1980's in the U.S., but made few significant inroads into the complex patterns of controls existing at all levels of government. Until more deregulation is accomplished, individuals who aspire to exercise their innovative, acquisitive and productive capabilities vigorously will continue to seek the few relatively "government free" zones for their activities. That is as it should be, so far as the individuals are concerned.

But by driving away interests and talents that would otherwise be devoted to subjects intensely controlled by regulation, government skews the fields chosen by individuals for their private endeavors. The practice of medicine is an example of a prominent profession that has lost its appeal to many bright, young (and some not so young) minds, due largely to the predominant and stifling influences of government regulation.

Whatever the field of endeavor to be pursued by an individual of any age, any person interested in advancement ought to be armed and educated with the most useful tools and instruments available. Today and tomorrow, those tools and instruments will include those that bring relevant information most rapidly, cheaply and understandably. Today those instruments include the personal computer and access to the world wide web, both of which can be had essentially free of charge. Never in history have great numbers of individuals had such power at their fingertips.

The power is in the form of practically instantaneous access to valuable information that can be marshaled for one's own purposes to improve productivity and to acquire resources. This empowerment will enable individuals to transform their own well-being and, thereby, the world, more rapidly than can be presently conceived.

Within the next five years, hundreds of thousands and even millions of the subjects of China will gain access to modern communications through satellite-enabled internet (or intranet) service. Russia, India, other Asian countries, Eastern Europe and Latin America are either ahead of China in this respect or not far behind.

The scope of the potential increase in the capabilities of individuals to advance their own self-interests through use of the new computer based communications infrastructure is staggering. One can only imagine the impact of *Wealth of Nations* in 1776 if the British people had the personal computer and the internet at their disposal when Adam Smith published his enlightenment.

Each person today stands upon a foundation of immensely rich resources amassed by the vision, creativity and hard work of all other humans, including past generations. Those resources are, in many important respects, freely available for enjoyment and exploitation without charge. The instruments for use in exploring, analyzing and synthesizing those resources are extremely powerful and likewise available essentially free for those who aspire to use them. This is an opportunity bristling with tremendous personal potential for each person cognizant of it.

Indications are that many more people are becoming cognizant of their opportunity each day. And they are not shocked by it, they are eager for it. Each individual first sees certain initial possibilities, and gradually sees many more.

The natural acquisitivity of mankind is being fueled by information and communication at a level never previously experienced. The fusion is just beginning to become apparent, and the light from this energy creating process will brighten increasingly into the indefinite future.

Communication of information will fuel imagination. Imagination will inspire creativity and innovation. Innovation will feed productivity. Productivity will feed acquisitivity and consumption. Acquisitivity will allocate resources to those most efficient in production, or acquisitivity and consumption will re-channel resources back to those focused on production.

This enlightened state of continuing progress can spread its wings from the technological and communications industries into many other venues of society if government and public policy will permit it to do so. The prospects for such an outcome, or reasonable progress towards it, will be improved by a heightened level of understanding and appreciation of acquisitivity as a beneficial characteristic of human nature.

Acquisitivity has withstood the tyrannies of the ages and is continuing the campaign to break free of current oppressions, with prospects for performing even more awesomely astride the steeds of light-age technologies. But if all this should come to pass, acquisitivity still will not be the centrum of human existence. The profound achievements and potentialities of acquisitivity are fully sufficient in themselves without misplacing this aspect of human nature in an overly exalted or misbegotten role.

Two of the pivotal events in that long campaign of breaking free occurred in the same year of 1776. The Scottish economist-ethicist Adam Smith expounded *A General Inquiry Into The Nature And Causes Of The Wealth Of Nations*, while the American farmer-statesman Thomas Jefferson composed the Declaration of Independence. One man's ideas launched a cent ury and a half of previously unparalleled prosperity for Great Britain, and concurrently counseled the world to the same beneficial effect. The other laid the foundation for the world's leading republican democracy while announcing the aspirations of peoples throughout the ages.

Such is the power of ideas articulated by a single voice and circulated from person to person so that all may know and join or dissent. Imagine the power added to such a voice by the internet, optical communications and related innovations spreading the word at warp speed.

One cannot have read and considered the observations of Michael Novak's *The Spirit of Democratic Capitalism* without becoming alert to the energy building within the populations around the world yearning to be free of centuries of oppression. Well before the fall of the Berlin Wall, signs were abounding that the sentiments sweeping the continents of the old and new worlds were not for communism, but for free markets and political pluralism.

Never was this more apparent than August of 1984, when the international Olympic Games came to Los Angeles. The boycott of those Olympics by the government of the Soviet Union merely emphasized what the athletes and peoples throughout the world had already grasped and firmly believed. Los Angeles was in 1984 the one place in the universe that captured the feeling: all things are possible, now that you're here![44]

The athletes undoubtedly felt it in their contests. The 1984 Olympic Games in Los Angeles were electric with excitement primarily because the location had come to represent in many minds the place offering the best opportunity for individuals hoping to do their best in their chosen endeavors. The Los Angeles experience surely persuaded many to believe with renewed energy that more governments ought to be willing to offer similar possibilities in their own homelands. The 1980's and 90's witnessed the flowering of new democracies centered upon free markets in the Americas, Europe, Asia and Africa.

The driving forces of acquisitivity in years past will continue to drive it into the exciting days and years ahead: the millions of individual souls yearning and striving to create, to produce and to make better lives for themselves and their families. The vigorous exercise of acquisitivity will have much to do with the successful achievement of those goals, but will not offer the total solution.

C. S. Lewis' conclusion that a person should strive to put all of the standards of personal conduct together in such a way as to be one who regularly does the right thing for the right reasons is very close to the mark. Such an objective may sound quaintly anachronistic and entirely out of place in a discussion of the human propensity to acquire property. To the contrary, however, virtuous principles are neither out of time nor out of place in a highly acquisitive world.

The truth of the matter is that a person who is successfully acquisitive very frequently recognizes the wisdom of the principles of virtue. The further truth is that, despite the apparently widespread cynicism reflected in the public media, many individuals aspire to live virtuous lives and, despite shortcomings sometimes most apparent to themselves, do so in exemplary fashion.

This is the type of person one might wish to seek out as a role model for emulation. Even if not a single person of this quality could be found, the endeavor to be such a person would be very worthwhile. Such a person could be asked for a fair evaluation of acquisitivity in human nature and its effects on society.

That kind of person might say that acquisitivity is not about greed, nor about selfishness. First and foremost, acquisitivity in human nature carries a message of hope and optimism for those presently having the least resources. Acquisitivity is a blessing for the poor that must be jealously guarded against erosion or dilution by the elite, however well-meaning they may be, who have preceded the presently poor in gaining wealth and influence.

Those presently having more resources may likewise be optimistic and hopeful, but acquisitivity requires of them the same as is required of the poor. A person is responsible for innovative and productive use of the resources at hand. If this responsibility is met, efforts will be rewarded through the multiplication and return of resources expended. Otherwise the resources will find their way to those willing to do more and better with them.

Each aspect of human nature has a unique function, irreplaceable by any other. Acquisitivity is as much a part of human nature as speech, eating and drinking, and sexuality. This will remain so, despite public misunderstanding or mislabeling and the repression that flows from it. The indomitable human spirit will prevail and success will follow upon success, particularly so with enlightened understanding of the nature and motives of those who create, innovate, produce and acquire.

Endnotes

[1] See, for general reference, Howe, Irving, and Widick, B. J., *The UAW And Walter Reuther,* (New York: Da Capo Press, 1973).

[2] **Novak, Michael,** *The Spirit of Democratic Capitalism,* (New York: An American Enterprise Institute/Simon & Schuster Publication, 1982), 14.

[3] *Ibid.,* 14-28.

[4] Novak, Michael, *The Spirit of Democratic Capitalism,* (New York: An American Enterprise Institute/Simon & Schuster Publication, 1982), 121.

[5] Novak, Michael, *The Spirit of Democratic Capitalism,* (New York: An American Enterprise Institute/Simon & Schuster Publication, 1982), 121.

[6] Wolfe, Tom, *The Bonfire of the Vanities,* (New York: Farrer Straus Giroux, 1987).

[7] Marx, Karl, and Engels, Frederick, *The Communist Manifesto,* (New York: International Publishers, 1948), 13-14.

[8] Fukuyama, Francis, "The Great Disruption—Human Nature and the Reconstitution of Social Order," *The Atlantic Monthly,* May 1999, 76-77.

[9] Lewis, Michael, *The New, New Thing,* (New York, London: W. W. Norton & Co., 2000).

[10] *Id.,* 80.

[11] Smith, Adam, *An Inquiry into the Nature and Causes of the Wealth of Nations,* Selections, Book 1 (Chicago: Henry Regnery Company, 1953), 23.

[12] Novak, Michael, *The Spirit of Democratic Capitalism,* (New York: An American Enterprise Institute/Simon & Shuster Publication, l983), 113.

[13] Smith, Adam, *An Inquiry into the Nature and Causes of the Wealth of Nations,* ed. Edwin Cannan, (New York: Modern Library 1937), 423.

[14] Novak, Michael, *The Spirit of Democratic Capitalism,* (New York: American Enterprise Institute, Simon & Shuster, 1982), 121.

[15] Davis, Margaret Leslie, *Rivers In The Desert: William Mulholland and the Inventing of Los Angeles,* (New York: Harper Collins Publishers 1993), 94.

[16] *Id.*

[17] Smith, Adam, *An Inquiry into the Nature and Causes of the Wealth of Nations,* Henry Regnery Company, 23.

[18] Wolfe, Tom, *The Bonfire of the Vanities,* (New York: Farrer Straus Giroux, 1987).

[19] Lewis, C. S., *Mere Christianity,* (New York: MacMillan, 1977), 95.

[20] *Ibid.*

[21] *Id.,* 94.

[22] *Gospel of St. Luke,* Chapter 12, Vs. 16-28.

[23] *Ibid.,* Chapter 6, Vs. 24.

[24] *Ibid.,* Vs. 31.

[25] Genesis, Chap. 24, v. 1.

[26] Lewis, Michael, *The New, New Thing,* (New York, London: W. W. Norton and Company, 2000), 259-260.

[27] *Ibid.,* 260-261.

[28] *Ibid.,* 264.

[29] *Ibid.,* 265.

[30] Lewis, C. S., *Mere Christianity,* "The Cardinal Virtues," 63.

[31] Lewis, C. S., *Mere Christianity,* 12.

[32] *Ibid.*

[33] Associated Press, *Tulsa World,* September 12, 1999.

[34] Lewis, C. S., *Mere Christianity,* 67.

[35] Shaw, George Bernard, *Bernard Shaw's Saint Joan, Major Barbara, Androcles & the Lion,* Modern Library (New York), 310-312.

[36] *Ibid.*, 237.

[37] *Ibid.*, 312-313.

[38] Drucker, Peter F., "Beyond the Information Revolution," *The Atlantic Monthly*, Oct. 1999, 54-57.

[39] *Ibid.*, 57.

[40] *ChoPP Computer Corporation, Inc. v. U.S.*, 5 F.3d 1344 (9th Cir. 1993).

[41] Lewis, C. S., *Mere Christianity*, (New York: Macmillan, 1977), 60.

[42] *Ibid.*, 62.

[43] Johnson, Paul, *The Birth of the Modern—World Society 1815-1830*, (New York: Harper Collins Publishers, 1991).

[44] *Los Angeles*, original song by Rita Jett and Wayne Jett, copyright 1991.